The World
of
"MESTRE" TAMODA

by Uanhenga Xitu

Introduction by António Jacinto

translated by
Annella McDermott

readers international

" 'Mestre' Tamoda'' was first published in Angola in 1974 by the União dos Escritores Angolanos. *The World of "Mestre" Tamoda* was first published in 1984 under the title *Os discursos do "Mestre" Tamoda* by the União dos Escritores Angolanos.

First published in English by Readers International Inc. and Readers International, London. Editorial inquiries to London office at 8 Strathray Gardens, London NW3 4NY England. US/Canadian inquiries to Subscriber Service Department, P.O. Box 959, Columbia LA 71418-0959 USA.

The editors and translator gratefully acknowledge the patient help of the author and of Maria Eugénia de Carvalho Penteado in the preparation of this book.

Cover art: *Carnaval I* by Angolan artist Francisco D. Van-Dúnen
Design by Jan Brychta
Typesetting by Grassroots Typeset, London N3
Printed and bound in Great Britain by Richard Clay Ltd, Bungay, Suffolk

British Library Cataloguing in Publication Data
Xitu, Uanhenga
  The world of Mestre Tamoda.
  I. Title II. Os discursos do Mestre Tamoda.
  English
  869.3 [F]   PQ9929.X58

ISBN 0-930523-42-3 Hardcover
ISBN 0-930523-43-1 Paperback

The World
of
"MESTRE" TAMODA

Contents

Introduction

Domingos João Adão, immortalised as "Mestre"* Tamoda,
is not just a fictional character, he is a living person, flesh
and blood, with hopes, desires and feelings, the product of
a colonial milieu with all its games, its forms of alienation,
its contradictions and contrasts. There is no one who does
not recognise him, for there is something of him in all of
us. He was not the first and he will not be the last example
of a social type that has flourished at various times when circumstances were favourable.

Towards the end of the last century, with the establishment of a daily press in Angola, there was a vast increase
in intellectual activity, particularly journalism, which lasted
into the first quarter of this century and was preceded, accompanied and even to some extent outlived by a taste for formal oratory. There were certain people who stood out because
of their rhetorical gifts, which could be displayed on a wide
range of occasions such as baptisms, weddings, funerals, din-
ners and civic occasions. This practice had its antecedents
in the old-fashioned soirée with its speeches and recitations,
and to this was added the influences of Republican lectures
at the end of the last century, the impassioned speeches in

* Master, teacher, general term of respect.

i

Parliament when the Republic came into being, and last but by no means least, sermons. All these fed the taste for oratory and rhetorical discourse.

Another probable factor was the large number of lawsuits that followed the establishment of the Republic and lasted right into the 1920's, over dispossession of lands. (See *Relato dos Acontecimentos de Dala Tanda e Lucala* by the novelist António de Assis Junior.) Native Angolans trying to assert their rights often had to turn to "provisional" lawyers. (This was the profession of António de Assis Junior and others.) Alternatively, they could conduct their own case, using the means to hand, which explains why in general stores in the interior of Golungo or Ambaca you could buy not only matches, needles and thread, soap and wine, but also a "letter", meaning one sheet of paper and an envelope, and loose pages of the Penal Code at so many cents the page.

The people of Ambaca are famous for their legalistic and complex mode of speech, and it is no idle legend. Rather than being a pretext for mockery, however, it should be seen as an object worthy of serious study. To take just one example, back in the 1930's Geraldo Bessa Victor, in his first work, an essay entitled *Poetry and Politics*, began by mentioning three great writers whom he called "outstanding luminaries of the pen". (I am quoting from memory.) Assis Junior himself, in his novel *O Segredo da Morta* speaking of the tailor Eusébio Costa, whom I myself had the honor of meeting before his death, piously transmutes his profession into "practises the art of measurement". Moving on to the 1950's, there was one much sought-after speaker, Augusto de Castro Junior, who got lost in the "floribundance" of his own adjectives and picked up the thread again with the phrase: "re-subjectifying the relevant question..."

Then there was the wife of a country doctor who was invited to lunch at the home of one of the local officials and asked for a toothpick: "Would you be so kind as to pass me a wooden dental probe?" I do not think we need any more examples to prove that Mestre Tamoda was not, and is not, unique.

This pleasure in words rather than ideas, in appearances rather than reality, form rather than content, was a method of self-defence, like the behaviour of those mimic-men who did not own a shirt, but always wore a jacket, or had no underpants but made sure they wore good-quality trousers.

Mestre Tamoda liked to reel off what José Maria Relvas used to call in his *Portuguese Grammar*, "adverbs implying that a conclusion is being drawn: thus, therefore, consequently, accordingly and so on". He was not to know that in our day these words would start to appear two or three times in one sentence, so that they have ended up as meaningless crutches and the whole language is infected by this "consequential epidemia" as Tamoda might have called it.

I knew Mestre Tamoda, and I still do. He is typically Angolan in his profound loquacity. To complete our knowledge of him, it would be nice if the talent of Uanhenga Xitu could show us the hidden face of Tamoda by publishing his collected letters and copies of the legal petitions in which he was so prolific.

I know the spirit of Tamoda is alive and well, for I heard it only the other day in a family reunion. The conversation got round to questions of kinship: "...don't you know that if a boy marries his first cousin the children will be illiterate?"

António Jacinto
Angolan poet and winner of the
1986 NOMA Prize for African literature

Author's Note

Agostinho Mendes de Carvalho...Uanhenga Xitu—this is my name, not a pseudonym. Everyone who saw me come into the world and grow up in my village, Calomboloca, knows I am called UANHENGA. There are those who insist it is a nickname, but the great Kinguxi, who gave me the name, is still alive and lucid, at the age of ninety.

Once I wrote an article for publication and signed it Uanhenga Xitu...Rejected. I was supposed to sign Agostinho A. Mendes de Carvalho. I refused. Either the piece was published signed Uanhenga Xitu or it would have to wait for the day when a publisher could accept the name by which I'm known in the village where I was born.

So the first literary work I wrote which was published as I wanted was in Cabo Verde, where I was imprisoned at Tarrafal prison camp. It was a few lines of verse with the word "NO", carved on the trunk of an acacia....

● ● ●

The story "Mestre" Tamoda was written in prison, where we were subjected to unrelenting surveillance and constant searches by the warders. My companions and I had confiscated not only letters from our families and other documents, but literary manuscripts which were never returned to us and which could never be reconstructed. Prison writing is the product of varying moods, and also reflects the differing opportunities for writing at different institutions. Moreover, whenever a prisoner is transferred—I myself was in four different jails—he is traumatised and depressed by the move, and is also afraid that what he has put down on paper may cause him problems when his belongings are searched in preparation for the transfer. Thus many prisoners tear up or burn their manuscripts, often with tears in their eyes as they think of the effort it cost them to write over many hard days.

"Mestre" Tamoda was captured a number of times. But in one of my transfers I managed to save the part that was subsequently published. When I was released from prison, I preferred to publish the story as it stood, though it was obviously incomplete. I think there will be no difficulty in understanding the character of Mestre Tamoda, either in the first short story or in the later continuation of his adventures.

The World of *"Mestre" Tamoda is dedicated to all my readers in Angola and abroad, and to the students at universities in São Paulo and Rio de Janeiro for the interest, understanding and sensitivity they showed in our discussions about my work.*

A word also to my beloved companion in life: one day I will return to being what I was, when I cease to be what I am now, for if I was called to be what I am, it was because of what I was....

"Mestre" Tamoda

TAMODA left his village as a young boy, and went to Luanda where he lived for several years. He got a job and studied in his spare time with his employer's children or the servants in the house next door. In this way, he learned to write a passable letter. At his last job, in the home of a bachelor lawyer, he spent his time when the boss was away on business copying out and learning by heart certain words in the dictionary that caught his fancy.

When he became a man and was ready to marry, he left the job in town and returned to the village of his birth. He got off the train carrying two large volumes and a folder. He also had two suitcases, a cloth sack and some other bundles which were carried home by the relatives who had gone to meet him. Arriving home, in the presence of all those who had come to greet him, he opened one of the suitcases to reveal a number of ancient novels, a worm-eaten second-hand dictionary, some loose leaves torn from other dictionaries, several notebooks full of scribbled words and two manuals: *A Guide to Letter-Writing* and *How to Write a Love Letter*. There were also some law books.

The majority of the villagers spoke Kimbundo and only used Portuguese on rare occasions, so Tamoda soon acquired a reputation as an intellectual and an authority on the language of Camoens and the great Portuguese poets. He called his dictionary his *ndunda*, which in Kimbundo means any weighty reference book. Whenever he sat chatting with the men of his own age, he would toss into the conversation, more or less at random, strange, difficult words, even for those who were more educated than Tamoda and could read and write with ease. If he was talking to girls who did not know how to read and hardly knew a word of Portuguese, he would throw in one or two words so obscure they were not even in most dictionaries at the time. So the village gained its own etymologist and lexicographer!

As he had come back from the city with money, he could afford to pay someone to do his obligatory labour in the fields of the village chief and other authorities, while he showed off his city clothes. This usually took place in the evening when he was back from his parents' field, and most of the field-hands were home from their labours.

Tamoda would stroll through the village, dapper in his white shirt and trousers, long socks, white pith helmet and two-tone black and white leather shoes which creaked as he walked. "Tamoda," the children would cry, "do a bend for us." Tamoda would saunter on, shoes creaking and head and shoulders swaying in time to the children's cries. He strutted along like a bush turkey, leaning first to one side then to the other, and smiling. Creak, creak, creak went the shoes and in time to them the voices of the youngsters: "Tamoda, please do a bend for us!" Finally Tamoda would courteously turn to his admirers, a smile still on his lips, and in his deep voice he would imitate their plea: "Tamoda, do a bend for us." Then raising his pith helmet slightly, he would bow like an ambassador. The boys, delighted with this gesture, would shout even louder: "Tamoda, again. Do it again, Tamoda." Sometimes they would chant in time to the creaking of his shoes. Then Tamoda would turn round and face them, one hand on his headgear, the other on his hips, wriggling his feet and wagging his head, wreathed in smiles.

He was immensely popular with the schoolboys, who were fascinated by his arcane vocabulary. He would meet them on their way back from school and they would gather round him in an attentive group. Some took notes on their slates, or on the cover of the books in which they wrote out the words dictated by the proper teacher in school. If they could not manage to get hold of a book or a slate in time, they would write on their thighs and forearms, which were just as black as the slates. Tamoda would dictate rapidly.

Then when the boys were talking among themselves, they would try to show off by slipping one of these words into the conversation. Naturally, this led to great confusion, since each one only knew the meaning of those words he had learned by heart.

Tamoda's fame spread far and wide, even among the girls, who did not always go to school. He would give out loose pages from the dictionary for the kids to learn by heart, which was much more popular than the proper classes given by the teacher, with his talk of diphthongs, syllables and adjectives.

The boys started to use Tamoda's vocabulary in their quarrels, both at home and outside, which got them into a lot of trouble because their parents and elder brothers, not knowing the meaning of the words, assumed they were wicked and deserved a beating. Take an example. One day as Tamoda was coming out of the bathing-pool, two kids asked him a question: "Tamoda, friend, what is the feminine of 'youth'?" Tamoda replied: "The feminine of 'youth' is 'maiden', in Portuguese 'muchachala'." He spoke with great assurance, happy to clear up any difficulties. The two boys, Kidi and Kuzela, sped off to add the new word to those already in circulation, such as lackey, lickspittle, dumbfounded, scoundrel, captious, pudenda, exacerbate, namby-pamby, hoity-toity, jocose, rigor mortis, zoomorphous, sylvan, hoi-polloi, buffoon, block-head, pilferer, ruffian, nincompoop, jackanapes, willy-nilly... Unfortunately, the latest one, 'muchachala', did not last long, for it sounds very like a Kimbundo word, 'muxaxala' which means rectum or anal passage. The boys launched this new found treasure at the girls, then the girls tried to slap the young Academicians. When they could not manage it, they ran weeping to their parents. So their fathers and brothers turned up to demand an explanation from Tamoda's young disciples: "So it's 'muxaxala' now, is it? Is that the sort of Portuguese Tamoda's been teaching you?" After which the boys had their ears boxed and were smacked and thrashed till they had completely forgotten the feminine of 'youth'.

They remained keen, however, on learning pages of the dictionary by heart, so that loose pages were at a premium in the village. Many parents were left with severely depleted tomes in this quest for knowledge, because their children would tear out pages from the dictionary and swap them for fifty or a hundred cashew nuts.

One night, Kidi and Kuzela went to the *sungui*, where people gather to talk in the evenings. Tamoda was sitting some distance away from the rest, chatting to Mufula, his fiancée whom he later married. Half an hour earlier he had chased away some youngsters who were bothering him.

"Hello, Tamoda," said Bento, one of his friends, "how are you?"

"I'm fine, sitting here with my betrothed."

"Betrothed, Tamoda? What's that?" asked Kuzela.

"I'm speaking about this damsel."

"What's a damsel?" Kidi then inquired.

"Same as a nymph."

"And a nymph?"

"Nymph is a young lady, a 'muchachala'."

"Push off now, kids," said Bento, tired of Kidi and his friends. "Stop bothering your elders and betters. Never heard that curiosity killed the cat? Get going."

"No, Bento, let them ask. They need enlightenment on this heterogeneous nomenclature."

"Fine, but there's a time and place for everything. They never leave you alone. You can't talk to Mufula in private."

"It doesn't matter, Mufula is not feeling libidinous tonight," said Tamoda with his usual broad smile. "Carry on, boys, ask anything you like. Tamoda's brain is an encyclopaedia." Here he burst out laughing. "Ask away! That's all right, isn't it, Mufula? Why don't you answer? Are you feeling a little unwell as a result of Sunday?" He laughed uproariously. Kuzela and his friends had lots more questions, but they were afraid of Bento, who was chatting now to Mufula. She was smiling at her boyfriend's indiscreet remarks, proud to be the fiancée of the village wordsmith, as someone had christened Tamoda.

Some of the boys who were standing around listening began to practise the vocabulary they had learned, so as not to forget it: libidinous...feeling libidinous...betrothed...damsel, nymph, heterogeneous... Others spoke again to Tamoda:

"Tamoda, friend, you should know that we've taken quite a few beatings over that word 'muchachala'. The grown-ups say it's a bad word and is not even in the dictionary."

"Who dares speak such calumniation?" demanded Tamoda indignantly. "I'll soon show them whether it's in the dictionary or not. The word-lists these jackanapes have are an

5

intestinal fraction of the reference books Tamoda consulted in the lawyer's house... What insolence, what audacity, what a complete farce! I'm surrounded by buffoons, bunglers and blunderers."

"Hurrah for Tamoda! Buffoons and bunglers. Great Portuguese, Tamoda. Carry on!" cried the boys jubilantly, carried away by their friend's fluency. "What insolence, what audacity, what a complete farce!" they chorused.

Kidi and his friends left Tamoda, who was getting ready to say goodnight to his fiancée and wandered over to a fire where some girls were roasting cashew nuts on a sheet of corrugated iron. The oil from the nuts made the fire flare up as though petrol had been poured on it... whoosh... and the cashew nuts crackled merrily. Occasionally a few nuts would leap off the sheet of iron and fall at the children's feet. At one point some fell by Kuzela and he covered them with his feet, but they were too hot to bear, so he kicked them to one side, intending to retrieve them later. As nuts continued to leap off the iron, Kidi bent down, picked up some nuts without attracting the attention of the ever-vigilant women folk, and put them in his pocket. Again, the heat on his thighs was unbearable, so he carefully threw the nuts to one side.

"Kuzela, give back the nuts you're hiding with your feet," said Sabalo, one of the three girls who were doing the roasting.

"Haven't got any."

"Yes, you have, I saw you."

"That Kidi has got some as well, give them back," said Kinoka, one of the women.

"That's a lie, I haven't got any, look if you don't believe me," Kidi protested, showing the lining of his pockets. "You accuse people of thieving with no evidence, you cheat."

"Cheat yourself."

"Shut up, you idiot."

"Idiot yourself, jackanapes, nincompoop," put in Kinoka, who had also picked up some of Tamoda's Portuguese.

"Nobody calls me a jackanapes or a nincompoop, you blockhead, you pudenda."

"Pudenda yourself, and don't give us any more of Tamoda's smart talk, just put the cashews on the ground, quickly," said Kamanhi, another of the girls. Kamanhi was a fighter, and already she had given Kuzela a push. The other children were jumping up and down, dying to see a fight.

"Come on, Kuzela, let's go, don't bother with these buffoons, these rodents, these imbibers," shouted Kidi recklessly.

At this point Sabalo's elder brother appeared, having been summoned to deal with Tamoda's disciples.

"What the devil's going on?"

"It's them, João, they came here spouting Tamoda's Portuguese, trying to steal our cashews. If we say anything they pipe up with a lot of rude words."

"So you come here with your Portuguese to steal, is that it? What sort of Portuguese is it, anyway? What's all this about rotents and simbibers?"

"Rodents and imbibers," said Kidi, getting ready to flee.

"Rotents or rodents, it's all the same. What I want to know is, what does it mean? And imbibers? That sounds bad. I've heard plenty of Tamoda's Portuguese, but that's a new one on me, and I don't like the sound of it."

The two boys pushed through the crowd and took to their heels, pursued by cries of "Catch them!" and a rain of stones and red-hot embers from the fire.

Next day, it was the reading lesson at school and three boys and two girls were sitting in front of the teacher on a long bench. While Kuzela was standing up reading aloud, Julia began to nod off.

"Julia is feeling libidinous today," whispered Kidi in Helena's ear. She grinned.

"Why are you laughing, Helena? Perhaps you think it's playtime already?" inquired the teacher.

"It was Kidi who made me laugh, saying Julia was libidinous."

"I see, you find that amusing do you? Kidi, who gave you permission to speak?"

"Please Miss, sorry Miss."

"And what is the meaning of 'libidinous'?"

"It means when your head nods."

The teacher turned to look for something on the desk against the wall, perhaps a cane or strap. Failing to find it, she interrupted the class for a moment and went to her home, which was nearby. Actually, she was taking her husband's place as teacher while he went to Luanda for a few days. While she was out of the room, the pupils commented loudly on events, pointing to Kidi, Helena and Julia as the likely victims of the day's beatings. Kidi was worried about his definition of 'libidinous' because he was not sure he had it right. His friends Oxai, Mbelengenze, João and Pedro, who had pages L—N of the dictionary, were not at school that day.

Silence fell again in the classroom as the teacher reappeared carrying a large illustrated dictionary.

"Right, Kidi, what did you say 'libidinous' meant?"

"Please Miss, nodding your head."

"Who taught you that word?"

"Please Miss, I heard it last night at the *sungui*, Miss."

"From whom?"

"Please Miss, from Tamoda."

"Well, I'm going to help you to forget that word." And the boy was cruelly beaten.

"Let that be a lesson to you all," said the teacher.

"I don't want to hear any more of Tamoda's words, inside or outside the classroom. Anyone found doing so will be severely punished, like our friend here." (Kidi was still squirming and snivelling.) "No more of Tamoda's Portuguese! No more time to be spent learning rude words instead of studying your lessons!"

After this sermon, the teacher searched all the books, folders, bags and cases, with the help of the older pupils. She found a large number of loose pages from dictionaries and notebooks full of Tamoda's vocabulary. There were no more lessons that day. As the kids walked home, they complained about the teacher's stupidity and the hatred felt by nincompoops for their wordsmith. Meanwhile the teacher had spotted in the notebooks a lot of words that did not figure in any Portuguese dictionary. Tamoda had made them up, and quite a number were highly suggestive. Needless to say, that was the end of Tamoda's evening classes.

It was around this time Tamoda was asked to produce his identification papers, for someone had denounced him to the authorities for not having his papers in order. He was already unpopular with the authorities, for calling the African police "lackeys" and "inquisitors" and Africans in the government service "simpletons" and "lickspittles." Then there was the question of boys fixing their hair to look like him. Quite a few had burned their scalps in the process, so that was another charge for parents, teachers and health authorities to lay against the village orator.

Tamoda arrived at the Regional Office in Catete at seven in the morning. He began to stroll up and down the verandah of the building, clutching two large legal volumes, one of civil the other of criminal law. They were leather-bound, with gold lettering and carried the stamp of the auction where Tamoda had bought them. A black strolling up and down like that, with leather shoes and a pith helmet, caused some astonishment. This was no ordinary person, he must be an engineer, or a doctor or a foreigner, murmured the other blacks who were waiting for the officials to arrive.

"Good morning, sir," said an old lady politely.

"Good morning," replied Tamoda, but he did not look at her, continuing on his way. Creak, creak, creak went the shoes.

This did not please the old lady, who began to mutter something to the others. One old man said, "I'm going to speak to him. I think maybe he's a local boy. He's been away a long time and he doesn't recognise us."

"For what? He's like a white man, the way he walks past us..."

"I'll ask anyway. What harm can it do? If he's a decent person he won't insult a man old enough to be his father."

Tamoda could hear this conversation as he passed back and forth, but he preferred to keep his distance. "I'm here to speak to the Regional Officer, so better not get involved with the hoi-polloi. Even the old man looks a bit of a bungler. They're so keen to be friendly, but Good Morning and that's enough. Imagine if the Regional Officer or his Assistant arrived and found me palavering with this lot! He'd lump Tamoda in the same social spectrum as them... he'd think I'd turned up here from a brothel, for heaven's sake. Nobody could accuse me of being stand-offish, but after all I don't know these people. I know they say that when a man is down you should help him up, but here we're all going to be down together, and there will be nobody to help us up. Better for Tamoda to keep his distance from the uneducated masses. It's different in the village, there everybody calls each other brother or cousin and any jackanapes can eat, sleep or dance with Tamoda…"

He wandered past a bench on which three African constables sat, and at that moment the old man approached:

"Excuse me, sir," he said, "I've been watching you marching up and down, up and down, and I think maybe you are from around here, but you don't recognise me. Can I ask your name and where you're from?"

"I am Citizen Tamoda, and I'm here in response to a summons from His Excellency the Regional Officer and Examining Magistrate, on a matter connected with my impressive mental facultations…"

The old man was none the wiser. He stood nodding in astonishment at the other's fluency in Portuguese. The African constables and some other people waiting on the verandah came over to observe the prodigy. Tamoda, however, the moment he had finished, turned away and began to walk proudly up and down.

"These boys, once they've been to the city, they think they've left the village behind for ever," commented one of the policemen.

"His Portuguese is first-class. He must have a government job," said another.

"Him? Don't you believe it. Usually it turns out they're nobodies. Next time you see him, he'll have sold those shoes and pith helmet to buy a handful of manioc flour."

11

"I'm not sure, the way he talks. He's not the kind to work in the fields or build roads."

When the Assistant Regional Officer and his clerks arrived and began to cross the verandah to the office, Tamoda swept off his helmet and spoke:

"Greetings, Assistant Regional Officer. How is Your Excellency?"

The other stopped for a moment, returned the greeting with a bow and went on, hiding a smile which his clerks nevertheless noticed and imitated.

"You hear that? Better not ask that one for a bribe."

"Why not, you already tried?"

"No, Corporal, I did think of making him a proposition but he has the gift of the gab and he speaks very good Portuguese. Black man in the Regional Office speaking good Portuguese, don't ask him for a backhander, maybe he makes a complaint, it's too dangerous, same as asking a white man. You don't remember what happened to our friend Kambengala?"

The office was coming to life. Typewriters pounded like drums and the people on the verandah began to be called inside. Tamoda continued to stride up and down while he waited for his turn, which was not long in coming.

"The Assistant Regional Officer says what do you want," said the black corporal to Tamoda.

"I have an official letter addressed to His Excellency the Regional Officer for Icolo and Bengo, Catete..."

The black corporal went off, then returned immediately to ask for the letter. The Assistant Regional Officer read it, observing the proliferation of comments on it, then he looked up the correspondence between the Health Inspector and the Regional Officer and between the latter and the rural authorities. Finally he smiled. "Wily rogue," he thought to himself. The corporal went back out to the verandah where Tamoda waited in his white trousers, poplin shirt and fine jacket. His black and white shoes, cleaned and polished for the occasion, creaked impressively. Disregarding his colleague's advice, the corporal was still brooding on how he could get a small tip out of Tamoda before the Regional Officer arrived. He decided to risk it:

"The Regional Officer has been delayed... but if you are in a hurry maybe we can come to an arrangement. We in the force (here he fingered his khaki tunic) are used to helping out all sorts of people, even whites. It is very hot here in Catete, so you look for shade where you can."

"Don't worry, rapidity is not of the essence, I wish to speak personally to the Examining Magistrate," replied Tamoda, and was turning away when the corporal tried another tack:

"You smoke? I'd love a cigarette..."

"Tamoda never touches the stuff, it is detrimentous to the brain and to the respiratory and nasaline passages."

Angry at his failure, the corporal went off in the direction of his friends, muttering, "Don't worry, I'll get him before the day is out. When the Assistant Regional Officer read his papers, everybody laughed. He's nothing, a nobody."

"Listen to the corporal, he thinks he's so clever, but everybody sees through him. Why try it on with this man, who's been holding forth in Portuguese since he got here?"

It was half past nine when the Regional Officer's jeep drew up outside the office. An African constable ran forward to salute and carry the R.O.'s folders. Tamoda, observing the arrival of the man he had been awaiting since early morning, drew out his books from under his arm. As the R.O. climbed the stairs to the broad, airy verandah, the African

13

policemen lined up to salute and some people who had absent-mindedly remained seated were ordered to stand. Tamoda stationed himself near the door, drawing himself up to his full height:

"Greetings, Regional Officer, Sir. How is Your Excellency this fine morning?"

The R.O. acknowledged the greeting with a wave of his hand, but swept on into the office without even a glance at Tamoda. Two hours later the bell rang: Brrring, Brrring. The corporal ran in and reappeared a moment later on the verandah.

"You, Domingos João Adão?"

"Otherwise known as Tamoda," replied the other. (Tamoda was a nickname given to him by the other boys when he was about seven, but he always preferred it.) "Your humble servant."

"What do you mean servant?" said the corporal suspiciously. "I'm nobody's servant."

"No, no, you misunderstand me," said Tamoda, "it's a courtesy, I often heard it said in the lawyers' houses where I worked: at your service, your humble servant and so on."

"Well, we're very backward here in Catete, we don't know much Portuguese and as I said before it gets very hot. Anyway, the R.O. wants to see you, but you can't take the books in."

"Why not? I wish to instruct, enlighten, inform and advise the R.O. with the help of these books."

"Forget it. That may be okay in Luanda, but here in Catete books have to be left on the bench. There are no robbers here."

Tamoda could not convince the corporal, so he left his books and pith helmet on the bench. When they reached the waiting-room, the corporal held open the door into the office and motioned for Tamoda to go in.

"Honoured Sir, may a humble citizen enter the inner sanctotum?"

"Just go in, and leave the fancy talk outside," said the corporal. The R.O., who was signing a pile of papers, had not replied, and he paid no attention to the new arrival but just carried on signing. There was no sound but the faint scratching of his pen.

"Don't fidget in front of the R.O.," the corporal suddenly barked, breaking the silence. The R.O. glanced up on hearing the accusation and the hand tracing the signatures wavered for a moment. However, he soon realised there was no basis for the accusation and went back to his task. Tamoda threw the corporal a threatening glance. He was tempted to let fly, but restrained himself.

"These educated blacks, once they've been to Luanda they lose all respect for authority. Get your hands out of your pockets when you're in the R.O.'s office." It was the corporal trying again. The R.O. glanced up again at the two men, then returned to his labours. Tamoda, who had his hands behind his back and not in his pockets as the corporal suggested, changed position and crossed his arms. "To think I worked for a High Court Judge, for generals and colonels, famous doctors from Luanda Central Hospital, all tip-top educated people and this half-wit of a cop, this idiotic jackanapes, this buffoon, this bungler, this bloody sepoy, this pudenda treats me as if I'm from the social spectrum... Okay, so the R.O. has still not attended to me, but that's because he's busy, not because he doesn't recognise the sort of man he's dealing with. Even in the offices of the High Court Judge or the lawyer where I worked, I did not speak until spoken to. This blooming copper is making a big mistake," thought Tamoda.

"Look, man, stand still and don't cross your arms in the R.O.'s office, keep your hands like this," said the corporal, pressing his arms stiffly to his sides. "Easy to see you were never in the army."

Tamoda cleared his throat meaningfully. The R.O. got up and went into the toilet, where he had a laugh to himself at the corporal's attempts to humiliate Tamoda, and the other's accusatory cough. While he was out of the room, the corporal went up to Tamoda and hissed in his ear: "You see how it gets hot in Catete? You people should bring cigarettes for us, we are not well paid…" Tamoda could cheerfully have strangled him, but he contented himself with turning away and staring out of the brightly-curtained windows.

The R.O. came back. "Right, let's see what this is all about. Give me your name and show me your papers."

"Your Excellency requires verification of my identity?"

"Never mind verification, just tell me your name. You've been denounced as a layabout and for not having your papers up to date, and apart from that the doctor was here and accused you of getting several boys a bad burn with that treatment of yours, thorn bark, cedar-oil and I don't know what else, and using a flatiron on their hair. Also, the teacher accuses you of giving classes where you teach rude words in Portuguese. I cannot ignore these complaints. You people bring back nasty habits from the city, then you go around passing them on to the youngsters…"

"Nasty habits? Me, Your Excellency?"

"That will do. For the moment, let me see your papers and we'll deal with the other matters later."

"Your Honour, just let me…"

"Papers!" bawled the R.O., who was losing patience. He stopped signing letters and stared threateningly at Tamoda. Then he stood up and again left the room.

"You beginning to feel the heat?" said the corporal in the absence of his superior. "The R.O. is only interested in your papers. Quit the fancy Portuguese, it only makes the white man angry."

"I have to put my case."

"Put your case? You think this is the tribal council? You boys get a taste of the city, you act like you're the R.O.," said the corporal, throwing up his hands in astonishment.

The R.O. came back. "Very well, say your piece, but afterwards I want to see your papers."

"Your Excellency, that black teacher is a caluminifier, and the rural authorities did not ascertain the preliminary enquiries on the hair question before sending in the report. It's a complete farce. They're envious because the kids enjoy my language classes. I'm the aggrieved party, under civil, criminal or tax law. Is Tamoda a lackey, a buffoon, a jackanapes, a half-wit or an imbecile, to go around doing these idiots' jobs without even being paid for it?"

After staring long and hard at the eloquent defendant, the R.O. signalled to the corporal to administer a beating to Tamoda on the palms of his hands. The "aggrieved party" could only show his papers from the previous year, for he had lent his current ones to a friend in Luanda to keep him from being picked up by the police until he could scrape together the money to pay for his own. (In those days no photograph was required.)

"Get back to your village now, and I want to see this year's money paid within the month. And keep away from the kids and their parents. If I hear any more tales of haircurling or pornographic Portuguese classes I'll banish you for a long time."

Tamoda went out to the verandah with red, stinging hands, to the great satisfaction of the onlookers, especially the cops.

"Well, friend, you see it pays to be humble when you come here. Fancy Portuguese is all right in the city, Master Domingos, not here. See what I mean?" said one of the cops in a bantering tone.

"I see what you mean, but I said nothing wrong."

"That's enough, grab your books," (Tamoda was having difficulty picking them up) "and do what the R.O. says. In a way you're lucky, you could end up in jail for being insolent to the R.O...."

"But I said nothing wrong, I merely displayed a little verbal dexterosity..."

"Stop, stop, you're very good with the Portuguese, but what about your papers, eh? The best thing you could have done when you got here, was talk to the right people, instead of trying to do things on your own. If you had slipped us some money at the beginning maybe we could have done something for you." It was the voice of the corporal who had joined his mates in chaffing Tamoda and could not resist one last desperate attempt to squeeze a tip out of him.

It was night-time when Tamoda arrived back at the village. News of his punishment had arrived before him and friends waited to greet him. I was there myself.

"Oh, the fellow beat me because I tossed him a few shafts of my Portuguese which left him stupefied... He was completely dumbfounded at first, and then he got angry because he could not grasp my meanings and beat me out of sheer envy. That's how they are, they hate it when anyone knows more than they do..." Thus Tamoda justified himself to the older men and his young admirers who stood around. "Right at the start, he didn't know what 'verification' meant. Then I slid in some legal terms." ("Bravo" was heard at this point from somewhere in the crowd.) "When I listed the various categories of law he looked utterly downcasted...he could see I did not speak just any old Portuguese, but the language of High Court Judges and eminent lawyers. So like lightning I threw in two or three unfathomable terminologies... Boom, Boom, Boom... and he had to give in. All he could do was beat me. But the person who's really to blame is that jackanapes, that pudenda of a teacher."

Tamoda died several years later and, just as the corporal had prophesied, he had been forced to sell his shoes, his pith helmet and even his reference books.

The World of "Mestre" Tamoda

Part One—The Village

THE NIGHTS were cold in June and fires blazed all through the village. Children danced round some, and at others people gathered to tell tall stories which were greeted with shouts and whistles of enjoyment. In the mornings there was humid mist or fog and as villagers walked to the fields this thin, cold vapour almost concealed the path formed by centuries of peasants' and travellers' steps.

Two teachers, one from the Catholic and the other from the Protestant Evangelical Mission, were discussing academic questions. They spoke, however, in such loud, excited voices, that it was more like an angry disagreement. Up and down they walked, up and down, in an endless after-dinner stroll, followed by a crowd of pupils and their friends. The precise point at issue was the correct way to parse a sentence from one of the textbooks, which went more or less as follows:

> *HOLLAND*
>> *It is a familiar fact that Holland is a country lying below sea-level, rather than above, as other countries do.*

"*It is a familiar fact*: first clause," said the Catholic

teacher, who had studied Portuguese and Latin and had nearly become a priest, until he was expelled for disobeying the orders of the Father Superior and because he was suspected of being over-familiar with the choir-girls in the sacristy. His name was Buíla.

> "*It is a familiar fact*: first clause.
> *That Holland is a country*: separate clause.
> *Lying below sea-level*: next clause.
> *Rather than above*: also a separate clause.
> *As other countries do*: final clause."

The origin of the polemic was a discussion at the *sungui* between the fourth-year pupils from the Catholic Mission and those from the Protestant one. Some of the pupils had alleged that the sentence contained only three clauses, others said four, others, five. One of the problems was how to link, say, *lying below sea-level* with the principal clause, *It is a familiar fact*. If the subject was *Holland*, why did it appear in a subordinate clause? When they took the problem to their teachers, the latter spent four or five weary days in sterile argument, which aroused a great deal of interest among the pupils but seemed unlikely to reach any conclusion.

The two teachers often disagreed, but this time tempers seemed to grow more frayed. Apart from individual obstinacy, they were divided on doctrinal issues, for only a week before they had launched into an argument about the status of certain books of the Bible. The one did not recognise the authority of the Pope and stated that there were sixty-six books in the Bible. The Catholic stood up for seventy-eight books, plus the Pope. What they seemed to forget was that these arguments, whether doctrinal or academic, sowed confusion among their pupils.

"Two of the clauses are syndetic," argued certain pupils as they went off to consult Tamoda on the relative competence of the two teachers, and how he would parse the sentence.

"Those teachers may have read a few books, but they're mistaken to the nth degree," said Tamoda. "They're puffed-up popinjays. You think because an eye is open it sees? Don't make me apoplexic."

"But, Mestre Tamoda, who knows most, them or you?"

Tamoda chortled derisively.

"Look, teaching is a job. Addressing multitudes is an art, and can only be learned from frequenting learned men and reading the books of High Court Judges."

"We hadn't thought of that."

"What I mean is this. If those teachers had to deal with notabilities, they couldn't do it. All they're good for is dealing with kids. Give me a couple of days, because they're talking rubbish that has to be heard to be believed. I'll soon put them in their place. This is a case of peripatetic exogmatism... I'll get my grey matter working and show them up."

"Peripatetic exogmatism: great! What does it mean?"

"It means people who walk up and down giving their opinions, trying to show they're smarter than anyone else."

"Peripatetic exogmatism, hurrah for Tamoda's Portuguese! We'll shout that out tomorrow when the teachers begin their walk, and if they say anything we'll tell them we're shouting it at the pupils who follow them up and down listening."

So the boys plotted to mock their teachers. That night, when the teachers began their usual stroll, the boys called out the refrain: "Peripatetic exogmatism", in a tone which aroused the suspicion of the teachers that it was meant for them.

Wherever they passed kids playing by the side of the path, the same words could be heard. The villagers, however, assumed they were directed at the crowd of pupils who always followed behind the teachers.

The two men were more or less in agreement that the sentence contained five clauses, but there was a big disagreement about the clause which went: *as other countries do*. One argued that it was an adverbial clause of reason, alleging that it expressed an idea of causality, the other said it was an adverbial clause of comparison. The other Gordian knot was the clause: *rather than above*, which the first man insisted was an adverbial clause of comparison while the other maintained must be a subordinate adjectival clause, though he had to admit he could not see any noun it could qualify. Since both had a highly developed spirit of contradiction, it would not have mattered even if one of them had been correct.

The contentious sentence was soon memorised by all the schoolchildren in the village and surroundings. You would hear them shouting it at playtime, or while they did their obligatory labour in the fields for the teacher, or picked cotton, or gathered firewood, or went to the sweet potato fields, or to the local market to buy fish, or to the fountain for water, or to the railway station to hand over or pick up the mail. ''It is a familiar fact...'' This caused a great deal of trouble with parents and older brothers and sisters, who complained that the children were all at it, and wished they might never hear the catch-phrase again.

But everyone knows that once children latch on to something no power on earth can make them let go until they get tired of it. A few cuffs may stop them saying it at home, but once they are out of doors they will defy all comers. That is just what happened.

Sometimes, to give the phrase a bit more colour, one friend would creep up behind another, his finger curled round an imaginary trigger, and hiss: "It is a familiar fact." The other would spin round to find the barrel of the imaginary gun at his temples. Trapped, he had to surrender and stutter out the response: "that Holland is a country."

Another trick, and this was one that really drove parents wild, was when the whole family was sitting round the table at mealtimes and some scallywag would shout in to his friend through the door or window: "It is a familiar fact", as a greeting or secret message. Sometimes the boy sitting with his family would be embarrassed and glance at his parents, not daring to shout out the answer. But it depended; other little devils would cheerfully reply: "that Holland is a country." "Psst," you would hear them say, "it is a familiar fact that the teacher's coming", or "It is a familiar fact that there's a visitor on his way". At football one boy would be dribbling and his adversary would call out: "It is a familiar fact, it is a familiar fact." And when they wanted to make fun of an older person who was a bit confused or one of those unfortunate simpletons who seem destined to be the butt of children's jokes (unfortunately such people exist), the kids had just the thing.

"Don't try to make a fool of me or I'll give you a beating, cheeky young son-of-a-bitch!"

"It is a familiar fact that you won't give me a beating." This was said from a distance and ready to run. "And it is a familiar fact that I am not cheeky and it is a familiar fact that I'm not a son-of-a-bitch."

"Just wait till I catch you..."

"It is a familiar fact that you can't catch me... Holland

is a country," they called, pulling faces and laughing. Even little three- and four-year-olds, playing with their parents or brothers and sisters would lisp sweetly: "Is a fa-miya fack..." And friends and acquaintances when they met:

"Hi, Joana, how's tricks? It is a familiar fact..."

"Hi, José, I'm fine. That Holland is a country."

Syntactically speaking, the words had become a greeting, like "Good morning", "Good evening" or "How are you?" Naturally, there were some who blamed it all on Tamoda. "It wasn't like this in the old days," lamented the old people, "when Oliveira Fortunato studied here, or when we had teachers like the Evangelical Pastor José Paulino or the late Manuel Antonio da Silva, Kundinda. Our kids were not so troublesome then. Where on earth did Tamoda get this power to bewitch our children?"

"If I so much as hear the words 'familiar fact' in my house, it's a good smack and a kick on the behind," said one father when the men were seated around the *kuseta* board playing a game.

"What are they talking about?" asked an old man.

"Familiar fact," he was told.

"What is that?"

"It's the same as 'everybody knows'."

"Everybody nose? What do you mean?"

"Don't worry, grandad, it's just Tamoda's Portuguese."

"Ah, Tamoda, that explains it. There's no one like him."

The Wisdom of Tamoda

MESTRE TAMODA made arrangements for a trip to Luanda. He sold half a sack of millet to pay for the return ticket, and he got hold of some eggs and lemons as a present for his friend Rui, from whom Tamoda had first learned to read and write. This was when Rui was in the sixth form of the Salvador Correia Secondary School. He also taught some classes in the famous primary school of Sr Ferrão, and gave private lessons in his home in the evenings.

On his arrival in Luanda, Tamoda went to greet some old friends and acquaintances who lived near the Coqueiros and Ambuíla soccer grounds. The houses in the city looked taller to him now. Lots of things looked different, the place had changed, there were lots of new buildings and streets. He went to visit the Town Hall, a place he had frequented in the days of his ex-employer, the High Court Judge, and where he was received with open arms by the porters and with ceremonious bows from the lawyers and judges to whom he had often served tea, coffee or whiskey in his master's home. The latter had long ago pushed off back to Lisbon. But all the porters and messengers still recognised Tamoda—so well-spoken he might be the old man's shadow.

Then he went to see Rui and explained the motive for his visit. He gave him a sheet of paper with the sentence that was causing so much discord and explained his lack of faith in the schoolteachers, useless idlers who were "leading the children astray with total misguidance." Tamoda would like to demonstrate that he was no ignoramus, so Rui was to put down on paper the fruits of his erudition, and silence those two dunces. They were void of grey matter, yet wanted to show off their learning!

Rui knew his ex-pupil of old, though he had expected that Tamoda's passion for learning flowery words and phrases would have abated. Not wanting to disappoint his friend, he promised to help and asked Tamoda to call back the next day when he would have a typewritten answer ready. Tamoda had not intended to return immediately to the village, because he had been invited to deliver the main speech at the wedding of Marajá, the nephew of an old friend, Bangu. Wonderful! But there was some hold-up in the preparations for the wedding, so another date was set and in the meantime Tamoda went back home. One of the teachers happened to be on the same train, and when it reached the station the schoolchildren who had gone to meet the teacher and carry his luggage deserted him temporarily and ran joyfully to welcome back Mestre Tamoda. Fully confident that none could now match his learning, Tamoda responded happily to their greeting. He began his explanation right there in the station:

"All doubts dissipated and dispelled. I was right that your teachers are a bit short on grey matter." And as they walked along the road he read aloud from his sheet of paper, dividing the sentence into clauses according to Rui's indications and adding his own further comments:

"Attention!" he requested. "Certain subjects and certain verbs are not stated but are understood. Pay very close attention. I'm going to read out the version arrived at by myself and my friend Rui, who knows much more than these supposed teachers, and as my friend Rui informs me that there are other susceptible ways of dividing the sentence, after each bit I'm going to read out my own explicatives, using my own grey matter.''

So first he gave the whole sentence, then Rui's analysis, then lastly his own comments, delivered in a tone of utter conviction:

> *It is a familiar fact that Holland is a country lying below sea-level rather than above as other countries do.*
>
> 1. 'It is a familiar fact': Principal clause, expressing the main idea.
>
>   Other clauses are subordinate to this one.
>
>   The subject of the verb is 'it'.
>
>   (The subject is *impersonified*, added Tamoda.)
>
> 2. 'that Holland is a country': subordinate noun clause, subject of the verb 'is' in the principal clause.
>
>   (Introduced by the conjunction 'that'—it is *syndetic*, Tamoda further explained.)
>
> 3. 'lying below sea-level': if we take 'lying' to be equivalent to 'which lies', we have a subordinate adjectival clause, qualifying 'country'. Otherwise it is not a clause at all, but a simple adjectival phrase.
>
>   The subject implied by 'which' is 'Holland'.
>
>   (This clause is adjectival because it *prescribes*, put in Tamoda.)
>
> 4. 'rather than above': must be construed together with the last phrase or clause. 'Lying' or 'which lies' is to be understood, so we have either a simple adverbial phrase of comparison or a subordinate adverbial clause of comparison.

(This is a *relative* clause—added Tamoda—because you can either put in 'lying' or leave it out.)

5. 'as other countries do': subordinate adverbial clause of comparison.

(Again the word 'lying' is *simplicit*, was Tamoda's contribution.)

For weeks afterwards you could hear nothing else in the village. It became a sort of game. One of the pupils would say, for example:

"It is a familiar fact?" and the others would answer:

"That's easy. Principal clause."

"That Holland is a country?"

"It's syndetic... syndetic..." the others would say slowly and deliberately. This infuriated the grown-ups, because the children deliberately twisted the pronunciation: syndetic... sundetic...sundu... so that it sounded like a certain rude word in Kimbundo.

"Which is the adverbial clause of comparison? One, two, three..."

"Rather than above."

"Subordinate adjectival clause?"

"Lying below sea-level."

"Louder!"

"LYING BELOW SEA-LEVEL!"

The noise was deafening. Tamoda's analysis was strictly outlawed in the school. The schoolmaster said that Tamoda's Portuguese was the product of alienation, and also that Tamoda was just a passing fancy—a mode, as his nickname Ta-*moda* suggested. As the teacher spoke he shrugged his shoulders, as if to imply that the other was to be pitied. But in fact Tamoda had shown conclusively that the sentence could be parsed as either three or five clauses. Weeks passed without the teachers resuming their evening walk, which was taken to signify their retreat before the superior strength of one whom they had never been able to stand—Tamoda.

"I should like to announce," Tamoda told his disciples, "that I shall shortly be returning to Luanda to perform the main speech at a nuptial ceremony for Marajá, the nephew of my internal friend, Bangu. He's marrying a white girl, the daughter of a very important man. The groom's godfather and godmother, Senhor Felix and Dona Laura, are very important men too. I am welcome in places where those two popinjays of teachers could never even set foot."

A Miracle

HE WAS a fine boy, Adão Simão; healthy, agile, goodnatured and the best football player in his year at school. He had gone to school that very day, both morning and afternoon sessions. At night he had played football by the light of the moon—the upper village versus the lower—scoring two goals that won the match for his team. Then suddenly that night, for no apparent reason, this young lad of fourteen died.

At the end of the football match he had talked and fooled around with his friends. He had said goodbye to the members of the other team. Yet next morning when his mother Kanzu hammered on his door to wake him, he did not answer. She went in and shook him, but by then he was stiff and cold. Horrified, she ran to the door, then ran back to make sure. Then she gave a cry, the longest and most painful of that sad day, which startled the villagers as they were setting out with their implements for the fields. No one moved another step. What weeping, what lamentations, what dismay! It was such an unexpected death. Everyone tried to guess the reason for such a cruel demise. Look at all the old men who were walking around with stiff joints and in poor health, some of them witch doctors—*they* don't die, but this fine young lad perishes instead. Who could be responsible? Who had killed him? Who had cast the spell? Possibly old Kimasuna because that day the students had pinched all her mangoes, she had put a curse on them, and Adão Simão was with them. No, it was more likely to be Kizomba, because last month when the boys were playing football, Adão Simão had given the ball such a kick that it killed the old man's cockerel. No, it was the boy's parents who had failed to keep the vow they made to buy off the spirit of their great-uncle Kuembi, when he was making all the babies die, so when Adão Simão was born they offered him as a ransom and promised to return again six years later, but times change, the parents went over to Christianity and forgot the old ways....Amid their tears of mourning the guests put forward all sorts of theories, trying to guess why the boy had died. They said so often "it must be this", "it must be that"; no firm conclusion could be reached as to why the unfortunate boy had died. There had to be a reason: "Death doesn't come and eat a person up just like that, there must have been a spell on him."

The dead boy's father, who was separated from Kanzu, the mother, worked for the railway in Ndala-Tandu. Advised of the tragedy, he arrived on board a freight train with a priest who was a friend of his and had got him his job through influential contacts. He came, all right, but he had to go back that same night, so he insisted that the body had to be buried that afternoon. He would not agree to the funeral taking place the following day, as the old people wished, partly because there were arrangements to be made, but also because it was blistering hot.

He also insisted that his son was to have a Roman Catholic funeral, which caused a fight between his relatives and those of his ex-wife, who had become a Protestant. There was a shouting match. "It must be done according to our Holy

Mother the Church." "The boy should have a proper Protestant funeral." It was not just the usual family squabble, on top there was a doctrinal conflict. Moreover, there was a third force, the witch doctors who would not accept that the church had any place at such a funeral, for the causes of death were way beyond anything the church could deal with. At one point it looked as though the Protestants would win, because the boy had gone to the Protestant school. In fact, on his arrival the priest was met by a choir of angelic voices from the Protestant Mission, which contrasted with the copious sobbing and weeping of the assembled mourners.

"On no account; I'm his father and what I say goes. I've brought the priest here; he's going to deliver the funeral service and that's that!" Whereupon José Simão strode into the room where—at the invitation of uncles, aunts and grandparents on both sides—the witch doctors were busy trying to divine the cause of the mysterious death, and angrily threw them out, to the villagers' astonishment. The witch doctors left in sullen mood, casting insults, curses and threats of revenge.

"This is a bad omen for the railwayman, a fanatical Catholic who is no longer our son, for he has foolishly turned against our ways. He has lost respect for the elders of his people. You would think he had come from Portugal and had never eaten the food or drunk the beverages of our ancestors."

José Simão's parents put it to him, that if he had turned against everything and everybody, it would be better if he went off home and left the funeral to them. Showing a lack of respect for the elders, and at a funeral with many people present, was like a slap in the face. "Even your mother and I felt it, as though you had struck us. Cursed be the death that brought these sorrows into my life. The old deserve respect," said the dead boy's grandfather, trembling with rage.

When it was time to carry the body to the cemetery, the priest went into the room, followed by José Simão and by the sacristan carrying a lighted candle and a wooden cross. Meanwhile the choir from the Protestant Mission, composed mainly of José Simão's school-mates, sang without respite, raising their voices as the melody was lost amid the noise of weeping from the mourners. There was a moment's pause to allow the priest to carry out the rites. On his advice, seconded by those present, José Simão agreed that the Protestant minister could also officiate, but he would not hear of the witch doctors being present. "They can do what they like, they're not poking their noses in here."

Then it was time to set off for the cemetery. Along the way, the choir continued to intone hymns suitable to the occasion. The cemetery was in open country, without fences, paths or straight lines of graves. First of all the priest spoke, conducting the ceremony according to the Catholic rite. Then the teacher, who was also a Protestant minister, spoke, praising the virtues and diligence of the dead boy and ending his peroration with his face bathed in tears: likewise his wife, Dona Elvira, whose eyes had been puffy from weeping since early morning.

Finally it was Tamoda's turn to speak. Visibly moved, he stepped forward a few paces, and standing before the coffin requested:

"Silence!" He waited for a few moments, staring at the crowd.

"Silence... Be quiet!"

The crowd was tired of waiting to resume its weeping,

which had been interrupted by the lengthy sermons of the priest and the minister, and they paid little attention to Tamoda's pleas.

"Are you going to keep quiet or not? Attention, please, do you hear me, blooming noisy people?"

"Shsh, keep quiet," put in someone from the crowd.

"Quiet for what? Are they going to bring the boy back from the dead? The heat is killing, out here in the sun and all they can do is gab, gab, gab."

"Come on now, keep quiet, this is no time for bickering," said Tamoda. "We see before us the corpse of an angel, with the mother's milk scarcely dry on his lips, a child cut down in the prime of his innocence..." But even this did not do the trick, some of those who were furthest away from the grave were beginning to weep again quite loudly and others were muttering and griping.

Up spoke Tamoda once again: "Honoured and benignant friends, gathered here today, I respectfully crave the exercise of your intermission to impose silence on those amongst us who do not understand the elevated rhetorical I must use on this sad and dark occasion, dark as the funeral shawl of this venerable ancient (here he pointed to an old lady), when our sumptuous oration rises up to the Eternal Father in the celestial heights..."

Someone in the crowd answered his plea: "Shsh, everyone." "Listen to him," said another, "then we can go home all the quicker, otherwise we'll be stuck here all day..."

"Oh, he's just like the other two, why doesn't he get on with it, this is really boring... if we have to wait around much longer let's just toss the coffin into the grave and that will be that."

"Enough! I have no intention of arguing with a crowd of cretins in front of this innocent corpse who astoundingly succumbed to a fatal erosion that befell him like a sudden catastrophe…" cried Tamoda, wiping the sweat from his brow with his right thumb and sprinkling it inadvertently over his neighbours. He wiped his lips with the back of his hand and continued:

"Honoured friends, gathered here today, the young boy, Adão Simão, who lies here in this amphora, coffin or funereal chest, was beloved by all and sundry. He was a pupil of mine at the *sungui* in the evenings. His was a cranium supercharged with grey matter and he had learned by heart many of my words from the dictionary." Turning to a schoolboy who stood near, Tamoda asked:

"What letters was he on?"

"He was on O and P."

"That's right, he was learning by heart words beginning with O and P. Sentences flow from my cranium, like a river, to carry to your excellencies here present my feelings of utterable grief… My question is: Who killed Adão Simão? Was it the sorcerers, deceivers who display false tears in this hecatomb…?"

Then Tamoda raised his arms, fixed his gaze on the sky and in a voice trembling and tearful with emotion called on the omnipotent one to show mercy and raise from the dead their beloved Adão Simão for whom they wept. He called in a loud voice:

"Adão, Adão, arise from the catacomb… arise now, Adão!" (Some of the youngsters in the crowd, who were listening attentively, hastened to write down a new word: 'catacomb'. Some had only grasped the 'cat', others only the 'comb' and could make no sense of it. "Wait a minute, he'll say it again,'' whispered Tamoda's pupils under the stern eye of the teacher who would take his revenge later.)

"Well, then, Adão, stay buried and alone in this wilderness, out here amongst the grass, with only the howling of wolves and hyenas, stay buried here, we're leaving. Well, Adão?'' he called at the top of his voice.

The crowd could be heard murmuring and coughing, showing their consternation, but also their approval of Tamoda's gesture, which had touched them deeply. All wept. Some blew their noses, covering one nostril with their thumb and noisily expelling the contents from the other onto the ground. There were sobs. Tamoda still stood with his arms raised and his gaze fixed on the sky.

Close by the grave there was a bare, stumpy tree which for a long time had held a hive of bees, and was now full of honey. Someone absent-mindedly leaned against this tree, not realising that the heavily-laden hive was ready to burst. As Tamoda prepared to resume his speech, something whizzed past his ear like lead-shot (zoom, zoom, zoom) and immediately there was a hellish confusion. MY! If you had seen those wild bees on the loose! How they buzzed around in the blazing heat. There was a dreadful panic among the villagers, and more weeping and groaning than had been heard at the funeral. Off they fled in all directions. The furious bees whizzed down and stung like buckshot from a hunting rifle. The coffin fell to the ground and the corpse tumbled out, but no one stopped to pick it up. The grave now sheltered the grave-diggers and several people who begged their friends to cover their heads with pieces of clothing or wicker mats. The grave that had been dug for one now held who knows how many.

Mourners arriving late at the ceremony spotted people

running wildly away from the cemetery, and without knowing what was going on, joined them and took to their heels, running back towards the village.

"What happened?"

"The corpse came back to life," cried the mourners in horror, running on to warn the village.

"What on earth can have happened to cause such a panic?"

"The dead body came back to life!"

Imagine the reaction of the five thousand villagers; they fled pell-mell into the long grass or over towards the fields. Here they met the returning field-hands and called out the news in a voice that froze the blood:

"A great disaster has befallen us!"

"What is it? Stop for a minute and tell us what has happened."

"It's awful, the corpse came back to life, it's started to murder people and now it's on its way here..." Everyone who heard the story threw down their bundles of firewood and baskets full of grass and joined in the general flight.

Tamoda was being jeered and pummelled by a few people who were still reasonably *compos mentis*. As he ran off, pursued by bees he cried wildly:

"It was the priest's fault. It was the minister's fault." He did not know whom to blame.

Thus reminded, they looked round for the priest and saw him leaping over ditches and tall grass, pursued by more bees than anyone, divested of his soutane, which he was using to shoo away the insects, and wearing only his drawers. From that day on he was known as Father Long-drawers, or just Long-drawers.

A few people managed to get clean away, but most people crouched on the ground within a radius of several metres from the grave, some covering their heads with parts of their clothing, others writhing and twitching in pain. It was like a sea of bodies, prostrated in some bizarre homage. Finally someone had the bright idea of lighting a fire with green leaves and stalks on top to produce smoke, which chased the bees back to their hive, which was no longer a hive; but anyway there they hung, clinging to one another in a terrifying cluster. When night fell, the villagers were finally able to bury the body amidst many curses, directed mainly at the dead boy's father.

What had caused the tremendous alarm was the fear that the corpse would take its revenge on the village. No inhabitant of the village or the surrounding area was left untouched by the tremendous event, it was like a blinding flash of lightening followed by a gigantic thunderbolt. People fainted, there were injuries, items of clothing were lost, children strayed, some kitchens caught fire and the domestic animals were agitated.

The old men attributed these happenings to the witch doctors. José Simão, the dead boy's father, disappeared, and when he was found he could not see, so badly swollen were his eyes. He and the priest were treated with local remedies by the nurses, once the stings had been removed, and after three days they were able to make the return journey. The minister and his wife were still confined to bed because of the vast number of stings they had suffered.

A Friendly Match

TAMODA did not play soccer, but he enjoyed watching the game and he never missed a match, no matter how far from the village. He was usually asked to say a few words before the game began, though some people objected to this, saying that Tamoda took advantage and tried to turn friendly soccer matches into lectures.

Once the team were invited to play a return match against Kibetu, which is twenty kilometres away. You can see how keen they were on the game, walking forty kilometres there and back. They were accompanied by a huge caravan of supporters, and the crowd was even larger because people came in from the surrounding villages. It is always a pleasure to welcome teams from outside, and the hospitality of the Kibetu team was legendary.

So as not to waste time, as soon as the formalities were over the whistle blew for the start of the match. The president of the home club, however, insisted that Tamoda should be invited to make a speech, as he had done at the original village match.

"I object," said the club's coach, who lived in Luanda and had made the journey to accompany some of the players who also lived in the city. "I've never heard of a speech at a soccer game—this isn't a wedding or a funeral."

"Just because you've never heard of it doesn't mean it can't be done," said the president.

But this did not silence the coach and, seconded by some others, he called to one of the first-aid team:

"Listen, you've been around to quite a few places, you've seen lots of games, ever heard anybody making a speech on the pitch?"

But the man's friend, sitting on the bench beside him, gave him a word of advice:

"Don't answer, let them work it out between them; if you give an opinion they'll only blame you later if things go wrong. The last time this teacher-fellow got up to speak, with the best of intentions, he got booted and headed by the lads and we all ended up at the police station."

So they argued back and forth, unable to agree, and the match could not start. The local youngsters were keen to hear Tamoda, whose fame had spread throughout the district and they started chanting: "Mestre Ta-mo-da, Mestre Ta-mo-da!" which finally helped to resolve the issue.

The whistle blew again and the two teams lined up in the centre of the pitch. Mestre Tamoda, as a visitor, took no part in the discussions as to whether he should speak or not... but well away from the argument he discoursed as follows to his fans, both home and away:

"Listen to them chattering erroniently, without the slightest expertance in soccer speeches. I'm hampered on all sides by half-wits. It's a basic lack of comprehendance."

It was agreed that Tamoda could speak, and he walked out on to the pitch, followed by a crowd of noisy turbulent kids, all pushing and kicking each other.

"Well, Tamoda, at the request of our supporters we'd like to invite you to say a few words, but keep it short, as we're late already.''

What was wanted was a brief exhortation, but Tamoda started turning it into a public meeting. He was warned, and some players threatened to leave if Tamoda spun it out for too long, as had happened on one occasion when it got so late that the match had to be finished by the light from bonfires lit all around the pitch. That was when the goal-keeper Manico got his nickname, Burst Ball, because in trying to save a corner-kick he gave such a leap that he lost his balance and fell into one of the fires along the boundary line. He received slight burns, but one of his testicles was perforated by a sharp twig concealed among the dry grass of the bonfire.

''Gentlemen, Presidents of the respective clubs and Players: soccer is not an excuse for half-wits to have a punch-up, the defence has no need to assault the roving centre-forward who always tries to hog the ball and gets in the goalie's way. If anyone in the august assembly has brought along spells to hamstring the muscles of the opposite team, I'd ask him to take his witch-doctoring elsewhere. Nor do we want any abusement of drugs. The linesmen are not to hold up their flag every two minutes, and the referee is to be like a High Court Judge, dispensing justice impartially. He shouldn't cheat, but he shouldn't poke his nose in too much either. I wish the two teams optimum luck in this challenge.'' He finished amidst shouts and applause from the youngsters.

Tamoda's team won, but when it came to the presentation of the cup, strangely enough the ''cup'' had run away. It happened to be a well-fed pig.

''Everybody look for the cup! You kids search the long grass and the village.''

They went back to the pigsty of the man who had sold them the trophy. Meanwhile the children set off to beat the bushes in the hope of finding it.

"The cup ran away, the cup ran away," they shouted.

An argument broke out between the directors and the players of the home team who were covered in shame and embarrassment. The visiting team's coach was no happier:

"Are we to believe that a pig could slip out of a rope that could tether a horse and amble quietly off without anybody seeing it? You're all witnesses, we saw it before the match tied with this rope to this stake. This is a set-up between the team and the villagers," he lamented.

"It can't be denied," said the president of the home team, "that this is a stain on the reputation of all of us in the club and even in the village. However, it can't be helped, the pig has got a head start, and it's getting late, we'll never find it tonight; so either we go and grab a pig from the first pigsty we come across, to protect our good name, or we swear to bring you a pig tomorrow."

"No, neither of those suggestions is any good. Keep your pig. A pig taken without the owner's permission could give the dropsy to anyone who ate it, and we don't want to croak. Getting a pig tomorrow isn't the same—the whole point was to arrive back at the village in triumph with a nice grunting cup. Keep it, it doesn't matter, we're the suckers. Come on, boys, let's go home," replied the coach.

While this argument was going on, an old man who had been at the game and heard the whole thing pushed his way through the crowd. He held up his hand for silence and spoke:

"It's quite true what has happened here today is a disgrace for young and old alike. A visitor should never be molested or robbed in public. Inside the village, it is a crime which pollutes everybody and which the spirits don't like. If evil men are going to carry out such a shameful act, they should take the visitor away to an outlying area and attack him there on their own, calling down all the bad spirits on themselves alone. To remove this stain from our village, I'm going to present the visitors with my pig, which at this moment is tied up in my pigsty, for the honour and glory of our village and our people.''

"Bravo, Hete," everyone cried with great enthusiasm.

Customs of the Village

THERE ARE certain beliefs and practices which vary from one region of Angola to another. Nowadays, contact with European civilisation and the influence of the churches has meant that some very good and valuable customs have become distorted, though seldom destroyed completely. There are of course some old practices which if they were to be resuscitated now would shock even the least sensitive person with a modern mentality. Yet there are so-called civilised people, even whites who "go native" and invoke African custom when it suits them. For example, if they want to marry a close relative, they have no qualms about invoking "tribal law" and persuading some elder in the village to grant them what they could not otherwise obtain, certainly not under "civilised" law. That is why we see blacks and mulattoes marrying their first cousins and nieces, to the astonishment of the old women who consider incest an abomination and remember that it was a deadly offence in the time of their ancestors.

Incest, in the sense of sexual contact between sister and brother or other very close relatives, is strictly forbidden in some regions of Angola, as it is in most countries and by most religions, mainly to avoid the risk of disability or ill-health from intermarriage. Some of our older people, however, tolerate it, though with misgivings. There are also groups who do not formally classify as close relatives: the children of two brothers, and even less so the children of two sisters, but that is because according to their philosophy and understanding, the fact of close kinship need only be stated where it requires explanation or elucidation, and in the case of the children of two brothers or sisters the degree of kinship is so apparent that it needs no definition—it would be like asking if there is a close relationship between father and son, or between two brothers.

As we said, there are rules, customs and principles accepted in one region but not in another. In some parts of Angola, it was the custom for those who had several wives to offer one, generally the youngest and prettiest, to sleep in the bed of a visitor. It was said to be to keep him company and warm him. It was a mark of politeness and a very great courtesy offered to the visitor. But woe betide him if he touched her! It was pure torture. It was also, of course, the supreme test of the guest's good manners and discretion. To turn down the offer is an insult to the host and gives great offence to the chosen lady. In a different region, the custom would be for the polygamous husband to offer one of his beautiful wives to his guest, in order to please him, in which case the pro-hibition on touching did not apply. Yet it should be noted that the wife selected was always one who was at the time of the month when she could not conceive.

Kazela, the mother of two children, was left a widow. According to the custom of the area, she could remarry, preferably one of her late husband's relatives, in accordance with a tradition whose main purpose is to ensure that the family retains close kinship links with any subsequent children. It can be one of the husband's brothers or one of his cousins, but always the youngest, because the oldest is considered a father-in-law. A nephew of the dead man may also "inherit" his widow, but only if he is the son of a sister, and he may be either older or younger than the dead husband. Under matriarchal laws, the son of a sister has rights of inheritance. Such cases are still to be found today, though not very frequently.

Kamixi (the name means "cat"), cousin to the dead man, proposed marriage to Kazela after six months of widowhood. At first she turned him down flat, because even while her husband was alive she did not get on very well with certain of his relatives. Then, as usual when there's a sudden death, somebody accused her of murdering her husband, and this wounded her so deeply that she resolved never to marry any of her late husband's relatives. However, she eventually yielded to the persuasion of two old aunts and accepted Kamixi. He went happily back to his job as a bricklayer in Dondo. He had been advised not to let the marriage or cohabitation take place until after Kuzela had completed all the usual rites of widowhood. Also, she was the widow of a hunter and therefore was bound to chastity. The wife of a hunter is always subjected to a magic rite whereby she swears not to commit adultery; if she ignores the prohibition, either she or her partner in adultery dies. If her husband dies or she gets divorced, she must carry out certain other rites to free herself of this magical chastity belt.

The witch doctor asked for certain items, which Kamixi brought along: a blanket, a piece of white cloth, another of calico, a bottle of port and a sum of money. He was not to return to the village until he was told that the spell was complete. Kuzela was taken out into the bush several times, sometimes by night, sometimes by day, to be washed and blessed, then she had to wear mourning for a time and only after that could she marry.

So the last days of the rite arrived and Kuzela was in a phase where she must not be touched by any man: even a simple handshake was forbidden for nine days. Kamixi, who had been waiting for six months, grew impatient and arrived one night in the back of a truck on which he had hitched a lift. After visiting his parents, he went to Kuzela's house in a frenzy. The young woman opened the window just a crack and explained the witch doctor's recommendations, and why she could not open the door.

"But you are my wife already, everybody knows that, so why not let me in? Maybe you've got another husband in there that you're trying to hide."

"Don't complicate things, go back to your father's house and we'll have a proper talk tomorrow."

"Well, just open the door to take some fish, palm oil and a few presents I brought you."

"All right, but you must promise not to touch me or I might die."

"I promise..." In he went, and by the smokey light of an oil-lamp made out of a sardine can, he gazed longingly at the enchanting Kuzela, more beautiful than ever now that her diet and rest were being strictly supervised by the witch doctor. Kamixi smiled, nodded his head, scratched it, wrinkled his nose, stared at the ground and sighed deeply:

"Aaahhh, you drive a man wild. So I'm just to stand here and look, like a eunuch?"

Kuzela, suspecting that the fellow might try something silly, said she wanted to go to bed and asked him to leave. Kamixi was leaning against the wall of the hut, with one hand on his head and his other arm between his legs. Above him was a shelf on which hens clucked and cackled at the cockerels. He stood for a few moments in this uncomfortable position, and then suddenly one of the cockerels shat on his head: splat! He sprang away from the wall as he felt the warm drops.

"I can't clean you, here's a cloth, you'll have to wipe it yourself and then off you go. I'm feeling tired."

"Alright, I'll go, covered in chicken-shit. Who cares about me?" and away he went, disconsolate and resentful.

The next day he set off on the long walk to the witch doctor's village. One of the elders had remembered that in these cases there could sometimes be a certain flexibility if one paid a sum of money to the witch doctor. The old witch doctor confirmed that this was so, but only in the gap between one part of the rite and another, to make sure the future husband was not impotent. In this case, however, they were in the final phase of the treatment and any relaxation of the rules could prove fatal for the woman. Now, if it was just a question of politeness, a handshake would be possible the day after tomorrow. Cursing the witch doctor and everybody else in his frustration, Kamixi went back to the village. He did not return to his job, however, but waited till the time for the handshake would come around.

"Let's face it," he thought to himself, "if it's all right to to touch the hand, it must be all right to touch other parts. It's all the same body."

So early in the morning of the day of his departure, he went to say goodbye, but it did not stop there, for he got carried away and Kuzela had to fight him off when he tried to force her by grabbing her and touching her in a certain place... The girl ran out of her hut screaming and alerted some early-rising villagers who were sharpening their tools ready for the day's work in the fields.

"Help, help!"

"What is it? what's happened?"

"It's Kamixi, he tried to kill me..."

"Kamixi kill someone? Is he drunk, or has he gone mad?"

Everyone ran in a panic to help. Kamixi, seeing the danger, ran off to hide. The whole village was now awake and commenting on the news: Kuzela had been taken advantage of, it was an abuse of trust on the part of Kamixi, who was he to ride roughshod over the customs of the area? Kuzela soon got fed up telling her story and reconstructing the crime:

"What happened, exactly?"

"He came in, took me in his arms and started to feel me all over, then he lifted up my skirt and touched me here," and she pointed to the place.

"Good Lord, what a thing for Kamixi to do, that's awful, that's a crime, touching a woman there when she's in mourning, especially now she's under this treatment, he could have killed her. No, no, he had no right..."

News travels fast in a village. The widow was Tamoda's cousin, and he heard the news being discussed out in the fields. That night at the *sungui* he joined a group that was commenting on the matter:

"Imagine this good-for-nothing," said Tamoda, "he comes back here with his white man's habits, in the twinkling of an eye he's got his paws on my cousin's pudibundous parts, he's stroking her hair and introducing digits. This is inadmissive, this is a crime punishable by imprisonment under Civil or Criminal law. I cannot overlook this abuse, tomorrow I'm going to lay charges. That good-for-nothing forced, violated, raped and deflowered my cousin." As usual, he was not alone in his lamentations, but surrounded by fans and curious onlookers. One of them interrupted:

"I admit what happened wasn't right, but I think we should sort it out amongst ourselves, the elders should decide what's best. After all, it happened in private between husband and wife, even though they may not be living together yet. Involving the authorities may cause a lot of trouble. I accept when you say your cousin was forced or even raped, but how can you say she was deflowered when she's already got two children?"

"So, Simão, you know all about the law, do you? You've studied with lawyers, as I have?"

"No, I haven't studied, but we all know you can only deflower a young girl, a virgin."

"Be quiet, Simão, you know nothing. You are probably a good-for-nothing yourself..." Tamoda wanted the last word, but the other man, quite cool and collected, was ready with a reply:

"I may not have studied law, but I've been to school, and deflower means take away the flower, and your cousin, excuse me for being so blunt, lost her flower the day her first husband..."

"Just wait there, I'm going for my law-books, hold on, hold on." Tamoda pushed his way through the crowd and shot off to his house, which was nearby, while Simão got ready to leave, saying:

"I'm going, he's welcome to his books, as long as he doesn't expect the rest of us to believe all that shit he's learned." But he was prevented from leaving by the crowds of noisy youngsters who spread across the road to block his path.

"Simão's chicken. Don't let him go."

"Bloody kids, I'll knock your heads together. Even if I do stay, what do you think your wonderful Tamoda can do?

Fight me? Put me in jail?''

"At that point Tamoda arrived with his texts, *Civil Law* and *Criminal Law*. The kids quickly lit grass torches and amidst a crowd of curious heads and youngsters jostling each other, the Mestre started to read out the definitions of *rape*, *violation* and *deflowered*, but he was interrupted when some of the burning grass fell on the book. "Quick, shake it off, it's going to set the page alight!" The crowd momentarily dispersed. When they came back, Tamoda had started to read from the second book. Without waiting to understand the definitions, Tamoda's cohorts were already crying victory and hooting at Simão: "Igno-ra-mus. Igno-ra-mus." Somebody did point out that Tamoda had only got as far as *aggravated rape*.

"Can't stop now, *deflowering* is in the other book. But listen, Simão, what about an old woman who's never been married, or even better, a nun, who is forced to have sexual relations when she's old. Is she deflowered or not?''

"For Heaven's sake, Tamoda, don't joke about things like that," said Nzangu, who was very religious and was offended by the reference to a nun. "Your question is disgraceful, infamous. I'm going to tell the priest and the authorities. It's an insult to the Church," he shouted, waving his arms. He was a middle-aged man who had been a native catechist.

Seeing Nzangu's anger and excitement, the group split into two factions; one alleging that Tamoda's words had been misinterpreted and did not constitute an offence; the other, like Simão, who was also a Catholic, refusing to accept this explanation. The angry voices continued on into the night. "Okay, get your shirt off and I'll teach you a lesson." "Oh, yes, you and whose army?" "Come on, break it up." "I'll break you up." Finally the old men who had just got off to sleep had to get up and separate the warring bands....

Departures

THE READER will remember that Tamoda had told his fans: "I am happy to announce that I shall shortly be returning to Luanda to perform an important speech at a high-class nuptial ceremony." This was the reason for his next trip to Luanda.

Knowing that he was to be an important guest at Marajá's wedding, he spent hours preparing his speech and writing down in a ruled notebook certain words copied from the dictionary. He learned whole pages by heart, in random order, that is, he would learn either A-D or R-S, wherever he spotted a word that he thought would sound good in a particular place. He even memorised grammatical rules from Sr. José Maria Relvas's *Portuguese Grammar*, though this served little practical function.

He then made his preparations for the trip to Luanda. He was to take some crates of lemons with him, and three large baskets of eggs, some as a present in case Dona Laura wanted to bake cakes for the wedding and the rest to be sold to the pursers and crew of the Portuguese and foreign ships anchored in the port of Luanda. This was during the War; lemons and eggs were highly sought-after and you could earn a lot from them, and from the skins of otters and other animals which Tamoda was also taking.

The day the train comes in, the railway station is the place for conversation, stories, disputes, family reunions and even impromptu trials if one of the local sepoys or tribal chieftains spots someone who has not paid his tax: an improvised court room is set up under a large, shady tree, and summary judgements delivered, with council and witnesses grabbed here and there at random. That is how it is done.

On this particular day, the station was crammed with people. Some were travelling, others had come to say goodbye, some were awaiting relatives from further up the line, Malange and intervening stations. It was a colourful scene, with crowds milling around and kids jumping on the lines until the train appeared. The flowers and leaves of mango trees and cashews exhaled a pleasant perfume, and the sun shone from a cloudless, blue sky, casting its joyful light over manioc fields with here and there the beauty of *baobabs* and eucalyptus.

Beyond the trees, a thin line of bluish-white smoke spiralled upwards, showing that the men were at work in their friend Kiahoji's fields. In the lush green branches and bending foliage of the fig trees, a whole world of different birds chirped, hopping from branch to branch, playing and looking for figs. It was a symphony of bird-song.... In the leafy shade of a mango tree sat a cluster of old men and women, talking about the harvest and giving sage advice to sons and daughters who lived and worked in Luanda. In another place, under a cashew tree, a group of boys and girls of marriageable age sat chatting, probably telling each other secrets, to judge by the way one girl would put her head close to another's to give her a last message for the boyfriend in the city. From time to time, someone would interrupt with the clauses they had learned from Mestre Tamoda: "Jay, it is a familiar fact..." "Right, Manuel, it's the principal clause, isn't it?"

One group of kids was playing *North, South, East or West?* This is a game played with spears of long grass. A child holds a spear by the base of the stem, moistens it with spittle and presses, while asking his question, and the point begins to turn in different directions. Another group played soccer with a bundle of rags tied together, on an improvised pitch of grass stubble.

A mother or aunt was advising Chico it was time he settled down; or asking Uncle Fernandes to do everything he could to get Kimba out of jail. "Why have I such bad luck?" the lady sighed. "Other people get parcels from their children, all I get in life is sorrow, it's my unhappy fate..."

On the other side of the road, under a huge guava tree and with his back to an ant-hill sat old Noka, absent-mindedly twanging a *finger piano* and singing a song by Mbuende:

> *Marry an old woman, you'll have to carry her,*
> *If one stumbles, both will fall.*
> *Marry a young one, she won't tarry long,*
> *Tomorrow she'll seek a younger mate.*
> *She'll scratch you and pinch you,*
> *Kill you by inches before your time.*
> *You cry, "Ouch, what was that thing?"*
> *She'll say, "Nothing, an insect's sting."*
> *Go 'way wife, you won't inherit my land.*
> *Your wealth is in that pretty place covered by your hands.*
> *You're born with it and take it with you when you die.*
> *Like the palm grove*
> *It gives you fruit and oil,*

So long as the tree is alive.
Go 'way, go 'way, wife, and hurt me no more...

"Listen, Noka," said a jolly old lady, "could you move off somewhere else? We can't hear ourselves speak for the noise. Who are you trying to impress? If it's an old woman you're after, I'm willing. But please go and play somewhere else."

She turned to her friend: "That Noka's a rogue. He makes out he's blind, but he sees what everyone is getting up to. He's also supposed to be deaf, but he hears everything that's going on and puts it into his songs." (Noka was a composer, musician and poet, a widower with no children. He was a simple soul who more or less lived off his relations and admirers. But he was a terrible gossip, and everything he found out ended up in his songs. He had trouble with some people, but how his fans loved him!)

Down the railway-line the switchman with his bugle in one hand and his flag in the other was shouting:

"Do not cross the line, the train is nearly here, it has already left Barraca. Oi, José, you little devil, didn't you hear what I said? You'll get yourself killed. Kimula, try to make that little monkey see sense, the train's getting closer, here it comes..."

The day the train comes in is a feast-day for the students. The schoolchildren who are sent on errands to the station are sure to come back with titbits of news, mischief, adventures and fantasies. Those chosen to go feel privileged and flattered. One reason the students love it when there's a train is that you can be sure of seeing a lot of girls from the surrounding villages. Of course, flirting in public in daylight is not the same as in the darkness of the *sungui*, but if you're up to date with Tamoda's latest phrase, you can at least command some attention from the girls: "Hi, Josefa, that Holland is a country." "Hello, I think it's a noun clause," she smiles.

You have no lack of opportunity at the station, but you have to be bold and take risks, for you're under close surveillance from teachers, parents, older brothers and sisters and grown-ups in general, all of whom keep a close eye on the actions of the young. Still it is the ideal place for flirting, and even with the teacher's suitcase on your head or a sack of sweet potatoes on your back, you do your best. Often these girls don't talk, but at least they give encouraging looks.

And what better place than the station to catch the truant who has sent a message to his teacher announcing he's ill? "Ooh, you liar, caught red-handed!"—then there's laughter all round.

There are no houses or villages near the station, only a sort of store which opens once or twice a year. But the day the train comes in, there are swarming crowds like you get at a funeral, a clinic or a public meeting called by the local authorities. When the train disappears, the station is plunged once more into a profound graveyard silence.

Looking out from the station at Kaxadi, the eye is delighted by the landscape. Behind the station are fields full of dark green maize, spreading out and following the zig-zag path of a lush palm grove which follows the riverbed. This is Africa, despite all its troubles, its cries of pain. What a marvellous sight!

In the distance lies the great flood-plain of Kaminha, which dips to form a valley (the railway-line crosses the river by an aqueduct) and runs down to join the other plains and valleys which empty floodwater and rain into the River Lucala. It is a long, deep valley, where the sun sets earlier than in the surrounding area. From it rise a huge variety of tall trees, composing a dense and pleasant refuge. This is the only place in the region as yet unspoiled by the headlong, uncontrolled chopping down of trees, creepers and bushes for firewood for Luanda, timber for houses in Luanda, charcoal to burn in Luanda. Other parts of the region, already damaged, will within a few years be desert. Then come the consequences: drought, poverty, hunger, mass emigration to Luanda.

By the side of the road and next to the railway-line one can see paths, trails, roads for logging trucks going in search of sticks for lath-and-plaster houses, firewood and charcoal as well as larger lumber for use in Luanda's construction industry.

One species of tree that has escaped destruction until now is the *baobab*, which proudly proclaims its centuries-old presence. These have escaped for the moment, until modern technology finds a way to exploit them for raw material...

The only other trees left are mangoes and cashews. All those species that are good for making charcoal, like the mubanga thorn, have been ruthlessly plundered.

The Kaminha basin, however, is an oasis where huge birds wheel about treetops that caress the sky. In the depths of the valley the little birds whistle and chirp in harmony with croaking of frogs and toads, the cries of squirrels, the hum of crickets and the harsh song of the cicada, all giving thanks to God for still being able to enjoy the cool shade and quiet of this spot.

Luanda has killed the rest. That is what happens to villages and hamlets which are near large cities: they are suffocated by the city's needs. And where men think only of today's profit and have no care for the future, we have the all-too-common sight of people afflicted by drought. Even now it's coming, partly as a result of the lack of trees and shade.

But let's go back to the railway station at Kaxadi. Seeing the smoke spiralling upwards from Kiahoji's fields reminded old Kimbemba of "da Ronca's black pudding". He recalled the story for the other old men and they all laughed till the tears ran down their cheeks. This helped to pass the time that day until the train came which was to carry Tamoda away.

José da Ronca was a Portuguese shopkeeper in the village of Ndondo-a-Nzele, and he also had fields of cotton, beans and vegetables, on which he employed native labour recruited by the local government official. He was one of those very tall men, with great big ears, long fingers and hands, a foot that needed a size 50 boot and a long throat that had earned him the nickname "Goat-neck." He went around on horseback, endangering the lives of everyone else on the paths and roads. He wore a wide-brimmed hat, cowboy-style, and a belt with metal studs. Being a heavy drinker, he could never walk straight, and he had a loud voice with which he constantly complained about his field-hands and his customers in the shop. He had a pronounced lisp and an imperfect grasp of Kimbundo. His face was the colour of a ripe tomato, some said from the drink. He cheated everyone he could, and was a very nasty person. One of his habits was to relieve himself in the open air, behind a bush, and his turds were coal-black and round, about the size of a sausage. The youngsters would all gather round to look at "da Ronca's black pudding", as they called it in a song they made up one night.

The work shifts in the field were from seven until midday and from two o'clock till six. That is what the men had contracted to do, and they were entitled to leave once their shift was over. But da Ronca got up to all sorts of tricks, alleging imaginary misdemeanours to avoid paying the full wage. He would give orders to the foreman, Adão João, that even if the shift was over, the men were not to leave until he came back from the shop or the railway station, where he sometimes sat drinking and talking for hours. Instead of midday he would turn up at two o'clock and instead of six, six-thirty, to take the roll call and note down the wages in a mysterious ledger. Naturally, no one was willing to accept these conditions. No bell was ever rung to mark the end of a shift, but the men drove a stick into the ground and when the shadow showed them it was time, they knocked off. Some went to rest under a tree, others to relieve themselves among the long grass and some climbed into the hog-plum and cashew trees. But when they heard the clippetty-clop and snorting of his horse, and the crack of his whip, they stood up again, unwillingly, and he would ring a bell and line them up. Opening the wages-book, he would call out the names and write opposite each one the initial letter of any alleged misdemeanour, all the time blustering and threatening all and sundry with a beating, or jail. As he called out each name and the man answered "Present" he would throw him a threatening glance and interrogate him as if he were a schoolchild:

"One: Adão Joaquim!"

"Present."

"But you weren't prethent when I got here. Where were you?"

"I went to do *kukusa*."

"Right, that goeth in the book. *Coocoo-tha*. THEE. ETH. Here, Adão," he called to the foreman, "come and thee how to do thith. When one of thethe men goeth for a pith, *coocootha*, you write THEE, ETH. Got that?"

"Got it, boss."

"Two: Jothé Kiambu!"

"Present."

"Where were you before?"

"I went to do *kunena*."

"Okay. *Coo-nena*. THEE.N. Think twithe before you go for a thit again, my black friend."

"Three: Manuel Kinema!"

"Present."

"What excuthe have you got?"

"I knocked off because it was the end of the shift."

"Tho, thleeping on the job. *Coo-theka*. THEE. THED.

"No, *kuzeka* no. I was resting in my own time, after the end of the shift."

"Are you talking back to a white man? Adão, take thith guy down to the local government official for a bit of a rub-a-dub-dub..."

"Okay, boss, you win, write down *kuzeka*."

"Ah-ha," said da Ronca, giving Manuel the wagging finger and the sagely nodding head, "thought you could get away with it, did you? Four! Mateuth!"

"Present."

"Where were you when I arrived?"

"The shift was over and I was resting under the hog-plum tree."

"I thee, climbing up the hog-plum tree."

"No, boss, I didn't climb it, I just sat resting my back against it."

"That'th enough, I'm not going to argue with you, I'm jutht going to write *Gajaja*, hog-plum. G. Five: Kithomba!"

"Present."

"A minute ago you were thitting on your bum over there in the thade, you lathy black thcoundrel."

"I was waiting for the second shift to start."

"Okay, well, that goeth down as idling. I."

"In that case I won't work here again."

"Thay that again, blackfathe, and not only will you never work here again, you'll get a night in jail and a good beating to knock the lathineth out of you. Adão, take this guy down to the official."

"Okay, I give in, write down 'idling'.

"That'th more like it, you lot want the white man'th money, but you don't want to work for it." Turning to his foreman he said, "Right, Adão, I don't have to tell you any more, you thee how to do it. If a guy is lathing around, or thitting or doing *Kukutha* or whatever the hell he'th doing, you write it down and at the end of the month it cometh off their pay. I can't thtand lathy people."

As he was leaving the foreman stopped him: "Boss, I didn't get this bit," and he pointed to an entry in the book.

"What bit? You people are hopeleth, I exthplain over and over again, and thtill you don't get it."

"It's this bit, boss. *Kunena*. Why is that C.N.?"

"Oh, you blockhead. Path me my flathk." José da Ronca, though he wore only a vest, sweated profusely in the heat, and had to keep wiping it away with the back of his hand. His flask was a litre-bottle which had once held naphthaline for killing cockroaches. It stood on a makeshift shelf and he had given orders that it was always to be full. He drank deeply and closed the flask.

"Right, let me thee. For *kunena* you write THEE.N. got it? For *kukutha* you write THEE. ETH. Ith that clear? If you athk me onthe more, I'll pith and thit all over you... and lithen, be very careful, jutht becauthe you're a black yourself, don't think you can do a deal with thethe guyth, if I find you up to anything like that I'll batter you over the head with thith flathk... okay?... get moving..."

We are still at the railway station at Kaxidi. A mass of swallows flitted and fluttered joyfully, huge flights of them frolicking and swooping across each other's path, flying low, some in pairs, dodging rapidly from one group to another, all chirping and chasing across the wide open sky above the heads of the crowd. It was a chaotic symphony! Other swallows perched proudly on the telegraph wires, chattering away in their special language, which old people assure the children is "Portuguese as spoken by the saints". One bird would suddenly move up closer to another, as though to pay closer attention, then another would move in closer as well, as if to ask: "Could you say that again, I didn't quite catch it."

Some were restless and flitted from place to place on the wires. One would whisper something in another's ear and the reply would be a peck and "Be quiet, you liar, you made that up." Another ruffled its feathers conceitedly, gave itself a good shake and pecked the wires. A neighbour pecked it in turn, as though to tell it: "Don't do that." An elderly male swallow was surrounded by a group of his contemporaries. Further on, two pairs were chatting, cheep, cheep, cheep, as though to challenge their classification by humans as "dumb" animals. Just like the passengers and their friends, the birds gave the impression they were talking to pass the time till the train arrived to scatter them with the puffs of smoke from its boiler and its deafening whistle.

It is the only bird the boys spare; it is a holy bird and must not be touched. The stationmaster and the switchman were always complaining about them, because they built their nests in the waiting-room, on the verandah and under cupboards and made a great mess. It is a bird which abuses its position, since it cannot be hunted or killed, and doesn't pay taxes, and it would build its nest under your bed if it could. "All day long it's the birds," the cleaner would moan, when he was told by the stationmaster to clean this or that, "and at night the bats shitting. This is no life for a man, between the bad pay and the blooming birds."

The puffing of the engine could be heard some distance away, and as the din grew louder and the ground began to shake as though it were an earthquake, all the passengers and their relatives began to fly around with loud cries looking for their suitcases and trunks. Then came the special whistle warning the brakeman to regulate his speed on the curve... tighten up the brakes... slacken off... and as the train approached the points, letting off steam and loud whistles of warning, it was ceremoniously welcomed by a ritual blast from the switchman's bugle: Tootoorootootoo! He sounded his instrument in a position unknown in any other bugler, his foot on the points-lever, his bugle clasped to his lips with one hand, his unfurled flag in the other and his whole body thrown backwards: Tootoorootootoo... Clear the track! This was his big moment. He wore a peaked cap with a badge in the shape of a train bearing the initials of the Luanda Railway Company, and a military-style shirt with pockets and a collar, but in rags and tatters.

Pandemonium broke out, with everyone getting ready to grab one of the emptier carriages, or any carriage where they could dump their luggage. In the midst of the chaotic movement, an old man who had been watching the train as it pulled in suddenly called out "The Lion, the Lion", and pointed to one of the first-class carriages. At first some thought he was referring to a real lion, but in fact he was talking about Dr Aires do Sacramento Menezes, a black doctor revered by all the black population of Angola who knew him or who, without knowing him, were aware of his reputation. In 1922, in the region of Icolo and Bengo, there had been an uprising against José Bernardo, an evil merchant and slavedriver who set back by one hundred years the social, economic and cultural development of the people of that area, causing untold damage, leaving women and children without husbands or fathers, stripping villages of all they had, closing and burning schools. The rebels were captured and deported to the islands of Sao Tomé and Principe, where Dr Menezes saved the lives of many by giving them medical certificates and requesting repatriation for reasons of non-existent illness. He also released many from the army by declaring them "unfit for military service" on one or other of the medical grounds then accepted by the armed forces. Some of these former exiles, like Kazuangongo, Miguel Gasper and others, were at the station that day, and they recognised the doctor as he looked out of the train window, wearing his monocle. They went up to him and asked:

"Are you really Dr Menezes?"

"I am. And you?"

"I was a soldier in…" and from then on everyone wanted to tell his story, if only there had been time. The word spread: "It's him, it really is him," and a crowd came rushing over to see the famous Lion—a great leader and a legendary figure. He left the window and came to the steps of the carriage. There he stood in the flesh, a big, strong man, defender of his people, typically Angolan in the colour of his skin and his general physique, except that he now looked ill. The train began to pull out, and everyone waved goodbye. The doctor responded with his own hand, which was strong when it fought, strong when it wrote, yet gentle when it healed.

When they got back to the village that night, old Kazuangongo and the others who had recognised Dr Menezes and thus incited crowds of people to run and greet him, were summoned to appear before the local official, who threatened them with a beating and a worse deportation than they had suffered in 1922. "He may be a doctor, but he's black and has no right to encourage crowds of blacks to gather and undermine the authority of the Europeans who were present. Do you understand?" This reprimand and the huffing and puffing of the local whites only made matters worse, because the youngsters in the village organised a picket at the station whenever a train was due, hoping to make the acquaintance of Dr Menezes as he passed through again on the return trip.

(The doctor aroused these reactions wherever he went. Waiters in hotels, navvies working on the roads, field hands among the cotton, the coffee, the sugar cane or the sisal, humble peasants in their fields, road-sweepers, dockers, fishermen, hospital workers, all felt different in that fraction of a second, their spirits were raised and they felt hope for the future... Sometimes Dr Menezes would stare at them attentively, as though pondering those famous lines from Castro Soromenho's novel *The Wound*: "...the most striking thing about the black is his passivity, his air of permanent humiliation and fear, his fatalism. Sadness was born in these lands.''

When he visited what was then the Central Hospital in Luanda—later it became Our Lady of Mercy and now it's the Josina Machel Hospital—one of the nurses would always pass on the whispered message: "He's here! Dr Menezes has just arrived at the gate." All the staff would invent an excuse to cross his path.

Well, Dr Menezes happened to be on the train that day, but the story of what he did for Angola will have to be told another time. It is certainly worth telling: if it had not been for him, not one of the deportees would have come back alive.)

Let us join Tamoda who was now on board the train, in one of those third-class carriages whose capacity appears infinite. One of the passengers who had got on at an earlier station was standing at the window, watching the view. He was half-drunk, and when he tried to go back to his seat he lost his balance and sat down on one of Tamoda's baskets of eggs. Splat! Tamoda exploded and a torrent of oaths came tumbling from his lips! The worst of it was that this basket also contained his speech for Marajá's wedding and a list of choice Portuguese words he had selected to make their debut at that function. When the man stood up, his trousers were soaked in yellow egg-yolk, which trickled slowly down his legs. Tamoda shouted:

"Oh, Lord, this is a tragedy, a fatalism, a catastrophe, a hecatomb, a disaster and a diabolical shame. This poisonous snake, this imbecilic animal has spattered egg all over my speeches." As he bellowed, he brandished the papers in the air, spreading the mess all over the other passengers, who were now fed up with the whole business. To make matters worse, the drunk man skidded in a slippery puddle of egg and fell into the basket again! It was like squeezing a lemon, the egg squirted out of the holes in the basket, under the weight of a man of 80 kilos with generously-endowed buttocks. Up came the ticket-inspector and the conductor, and the latter addressed Tamoda:

"What, may I ask is the hullaballo all about? Are you the cause of the trouble?"

"No, Mister Conductor, what happened was that this jackanapes parked his bum on my basket of eggs and transmogrified them into this puddle."

It was not clear whether the conductor understood, but he calmed things down in the carriage, except for Tamoda, who feared his big day was spoilt. The man who was covered in egg started to make his way to the other end of the carriage, but his way was blocked:

"Keep away from us, you dirty beast. Go and clean yourself up in the toilet."

"How can I?" he bawled in his embarrassment.

"By putting one foot in front of the other!"

Voices arose from other parts of the carriage:

"No chance, he's not coming through here, he'll get us all dirty. He can clean himself up where he is."

"Look at the filthy creature, he's a pigsty," said Tamoda, and he continued to moan and lament for the rest of the trip, gesticulating and pronouncing his extraordinary Portuguese, which astonished the other passengers. He swore he would not let the other man off the train unless and until he had duly and adequately compensated his victim under the terms of the appropriate Article of the Penal Code.

Part Two—The Town

TAMODA'S FRIEND, Bangu, had also left the countryside for Luanda at an early age, but unlike Tamoda he never went back to his native village. Fairly soon after his arrival in Luanda he was engaged on the recommendation of the cook as a nurse or childminder in the home of Sr Pinto. This Sr Pinto was very well-known and highly influential in Luanda, and happened to be a director of a popular multi-racial soccer club and sports centre. The family took a fancy to Bangu and he was quickly accepted as a member of the household. Whereas at first it had been "Boy!" or "Hey, you!" soon it was "Bangu, come here," or "Bangu, go and tell Dona Ana..." Apart from being very high up in the colonial administration, Sr Pinto owned houses and livestock on the outskirts of the city. He was invited to all the best dances and parties in Luanda, and was even an honoured guest at Government House on great occasions.

In his first few months in Luanda, before he had found steady work, Bangu made friends with Tamoda, who was a bit older and saved him once from a beating by some obstreperous youths after a soccer match at Os Coqueiros. Tamoda took Bangu to his employer's house and offered him leftovers from the kitchen, and since that day Bangu had been eternally grateful and often visited Tamoda at his employer's house. Many years had passed since then, but they were still firm friends, more like brothers, in fact.

Bangu was put in charge of Sr Pinto's sports club, having been placed there originally as a porter, but doing his job so well that gradually certain tasks, even some written ones, were entrusted to him. He won the friendship and respect not only of instructors in charge of the different sections of the club, but also of the athletes and players who frequented it. Soon he was given the keys to rooms containing valuable equipment. He became the mainstay of the club's activities, since he knew the inventory of all the equipment for soccer, tennis, gymnastics and so on. He took in the subscriptions, sent out the notices and met with other clubs and official sporting organisations. He also carried around on his back or on his head piles of heavy sports equipment, jugs of water and sacks of oranges for the teams.

The girls who went to practice gymnastics adored him, for besides being pleasant and courteous, he defended them from the brash behaviour of some of the boys. Woe betide a player who did not belong to the club and made eyes at one of his girls! It was one of the methods he used to tempt in good players from other clubs. "If you have your eye on Filo, join the club—I've got the application form here. Otherwise, forget it," he would threaten. Such was the atmosphere of trust, that he sometimes went into the girls' dressing room or showers unannounced: "Ooh, Bangu, Mr Bangu, that's naughty, you should have knocked!" Taken by surprise, the girls would try to cover themselves up as best they could with their hands, towels or items of clothing, giggling as they did so.

"Yes, yes, I beg your pardon, but how else am I to find out who's pinching my things? Don't worry about me, I'm old enough to be your father or your grandfather.''

"Good heavens, have some decency, Bangu. Who ever heard of a father or grandfather seeing his daughter or grand-daughter in the nude!''

"Don't talk to me about decency, it was your own mothers who said I could go into the showers to keep an eye on you, wasn't it?'' And Bangu laughed, enjoying the sight of the girls under the shower, like mermaids with their long hair plastered to their firm, round breasts and bellies. But that was as far as it went, because he was a kind and considerate man. "Good old Bangu, isn't he a dear, isn't he sweet,'' the girls would say in delight. He was their confidant, keeper of secrets, carrier of many a love letter and patcher-up of lovers' quarrels.

It got to be too much work for one man, so he asked the directors if he could have some help. Yes, he could, so long as he got somebody honest, not one of those hooligans who would sell the footballs and pocket the subscription money. "Get us somebody like yourself.'' So Bangu got one of his nephews, Marajá, who had arrived from the countryside and did not have a steady job. Tamoda was still in Luanda when he first arrived. Marajá too came to rely on Tamoda's employer's leftovers, so when Tamoda left the city the boy had a hard time. That was what made his uncle try to get him into the club.

The Match

MARAJÁ was now sixteen. He worked hard at the club, like his uncle, and won the respect of the young athletes. He enjoyed ping-pong and tennis, which he practised with the players and coaches from the club, becoming good enough to challenge some of the best players. He was also given some coaching by a Liberian, a good player and one of the English-speaking Africans manning the oceanic cable transmitters located at British Consulate. All this experience was not in vain, for Marajá was asked to coach the novices in his spare time. Boys and girls flocked to his lessons, and after the classes some of the girls would stay on to pick up a few more tips from him.

Preparations were beginning for the tennis and ping-pong championships, which were both played in July. The competitors came from the districts of Benguela, Moçamedes and Malange. Only members of the high society took part, top government officials and their wives, Portuguese Army and Naval officers, foreigners from the British and Belgian Consulates and some invited guests from Cape Town in South Africa. There were also some students from the Salvador Correia High School. In ping-pong, there was one championship for clubs and another for individual players. The sport was dying, from the point of view of numbers of spectators, but for this championship there was to be a big crowd, because of the publicity and the interest aroused. Some of our leading black and mulatto sportsmen did take part: Diogo Caricoco, Columbano Peres, Saldanha Palhares and some others I do not remember; but just for practice.

Tennis was also mainly for whites, with the odd mulatto from the Sporting (another more élite Luanda club) being allowed to compete in the regional championship. No blacks, especially if there were foreigners competing, such as Belgians, British or South Africans. Of course the Sporting Club was overtly racist, it would not admit blacks except to the soccer team, and only admitted mulattoes after close scrutiny of their social circumstances and status. The blacks who played soccer there had the souls of white men, and the mulattoes were trying to pass for white. ''Sporting Club types'': the term has passed into our language, and a lot more could be written about them...

Many of the High School students were members of Sr Pinto's club and took lessons from Marajá. One in particular was a great friend of his: Arlete, the seventeen-year-old daughter of Sr Pinto. She was a clever girl and the prettiest thing you ever saw. Everything about her was appealing; the way she stood, walked, or ran, and her glance, for she had a calm, sweet, tender, sensual look, astute yet without malice, which was striking and hard to resist. She had a delicate nose and fine lips which had never sinned yet invited to sin. She was the fourth of Sr Pinto and Dona Amélia's six children.

Being very keen on ping-pong, Arlete managed with the help of Marajá's coaching to beat all her friends at the High School and in the club. So she would often stay on at the club ping-ponging with Marajá: ping-ping, pong-pong, ping here, pong there, another ping, another pong. None of her friends could touch her at tennis either, for she was alert to the serves and quick to stop them and send them back.

She wore a white shirt with blue stripes round the collar and the edge of the sleeves. When she turned round you could see the fastening of her bra. Above her left breast was embroidered her name: Arlete. She wore gold earrings and at her neck a gold chain with a crucifix; a short, pleated white skirt with a blue stripe; white gym shoes and short white socks. She had beautiful legs and thighs, and altogether a figure to which only a sculptor could do justice. Her hair was long and tied up behind with a bow made of lots of tiny ribbons. When she threw the ball in the air, or made an energetic movement, her skirt would fan out to give a glimpse of her panties and her innocent thighs. When she jumped, her breasts bounced and when she waited with arms and racquet hanging down, alert to the direction in which her opponent would hit the ball, she was like a sweet little monkey. She danced on the spot, like a boxer.

In one of the preliminary rounds of the championship, before hundreds of spectators, Arlete managed to do something quite difficult. As she made a spectacular leap into the air, she lost her balance, yet she managed to slam the ball over the net before falling flat on the ground. It was the vital point needed for victory, and the match ended amidst wild applause and shouts of "Bravo". It was a proud moment for Sr Pinto and Dona Amélia, and even for Marajá. Arlete was not hurt, just slightly scratched.

Then on the first day of the championship proper, Arlete beat her South African opponent by a wide margin. As soon as the match was over, she astonished her parents and others who were going to congratulate her by running to where the barefoot African servants sat and giving Marajá a hug, saying,

"It's your victory, Marajá, not mine," and then another hug. This displeased a number of people, especially among the South Africans and Belgians.

She won set after set in the following matches, attracting the attention of the visitors. One of the foreigners approached Marajá with the offer of a job. The skill he had shown in the training sessions, right up to the eve of the championship match, prompted the unanimous opinion that he had a great future in sport at an international level. The problem was that Marajá was not an assimilated Portuguese citizen, he paid the native caste tax, which together with other circumstances condemned the youngster to a future as a coach, nothing more.

After the championship, what with Arlete and her schoolfriends' victories over some of the foreigners and weaker players from the other districts, young people flocked to Marajá for tennis lessons. To keep her hand in, Arlete continued her lessons in tennis and ping-pong. There was more freedom now in her conversation and relations with Marajá, they treated each other as friends, whereas before it had been "Miss Arlete, hit the ball this way," or "Hold the racquet like that, Miss Arlete". Perhaps she felt more at ease, because of the praise she was receiving from all sides. Marajá had been very shy and inhibited at first, knowing she was Sr Pinto's daughter, but as they ping-ponged away he began to say "Run, Arlete," or "Arlete, twist your racquet", when there were not many people around, and when they were completely alone he would sometimes put a hand on her shoulder to correct an awkward movement. She seemed quite happy, and never looked as if she minded, in fact she appeared to welcome what was happening. Marajá had won her parents' trust and had been asked to see her home if the class finished late.

Their intimacy grew as time passed, for the ping-pong classes continued throughout the year. On one occasion the lesson was on a Sunday afternoon. The game continued beyond the usual time, till there was no longer anyone else around. In the trophy room there was not a soul to be seen, and only the photograph of old players and members of the club could spy on them as they sat down to rest on a pile of equipment. A mouse scuttled past, followed by a white beetle, which Arlete had never seen before, so she ran after it. As it was too fast for her, she asked Marajá to join the hunt. She wanted to catch it alive and take it to her science class in the High School next day. As they ran hither and thither, either by chance or design, they coincided at a corner of a billiard table which stood in the centre of the room, and their bodies collided in an embrace that made Marajá tingle. Arlete was smiling. No, she wasn't hurt, no damage had been done. When they caught the beetle, they sat down again on the bundles, panting from the chase, and suddenly, without premeditation, without a word, without even a gesture, they found themselves lying down together locked in an embrace.

"Please be careful, do be careful, you're hurting me, Marajá. Oh, look at that. Look what you've done."

"It's nothing, you can wipe it away with your blouse."

On the way from the club to the house, Arlete felt like a different person. Marajá took his leave near the house and pensively went back to the club. So, not only was he young, athletic, powerful and fit, he was like the Greek athletes of old, not only good at tennis and ping-pong, but virile, a man.

He was a bit worried, admittedly, about what would happen if they were found out.

Arlete went in and made straight for the bathroom, naturally. She had a bath and threw her shorts and other clothes in the dirty linen basket. She did not sleep very soundly, after her strange experience. "I had no idea," she thought to herself, "it's just a physical exercise like any other." The next day she felt tired and she had a headache and stomach ache, so she stayed in bed and told her mother she could not go to school, but to please take care of the white beetle.

As usual on Mondays, the housekeeper went from room to room collecting the dirty clothing, checking it, noting down each garment and sending it to be washed. In Arlete's room she found the shorts stained with blood, special blood, virgin blood, which drew the housekeeper's attention. She inspected the girl's panties, too. This black matron, Josefa, was very Portuguesified, having been a servant in great houses, to heads of banks and lawyers. She spoke with extreme care, imitating the formal speech of the white ladies who lived in the great houses. Being a tremendous gossip, she was not going to ignore her findings. She stood plunged in thought for a moment, then she sighed: "Hmmm." She put to one side the clothing stained from the "physical exercise" and bundled up the rest for the washerwoman, Domingas.

This Domingas had a large family of daughters and was well-known and oft-consulted as a checker or investigator of girls who might have strayed from the straight and narrow. People had so much faith in her examinations, performed by introducing eggs of various sizes into the vagina, that they were accepted by some doctors and even by some courts of law.

"Off you go to old Domingas and don't come bothering me, I've more to do with my time," certain doctors would say, only half in jest, to mothers and fathers who were trying to find out if their daughters were still intact.

"Well, have you been to old Domingas yet? What did she use for your daughter? An egg from a duck, a hen, a bantam or a pigeon?" It was true that this strange personage did keep a stock of different-sized eggs. The pointed end of a partridge's egg was her favourite, it never lied, in fact with her skill from years of experience the old woman could sometimes even give the date of the deflowering.

One morning, for example, they brought her a sheet which had been stained with blood and then put away, several years before. It was now to be produced on the day after a wedding night, to be examined by the relatives on both sides. The problem was that the groom was doubtful, he could not remember if he had in fact been responsible for the vital act five years previously, and, unwilling to take his bride's word for it had sought the help of Domingas through some of his aunts. A few hours after receiving the sheet, Domingas called on the groom's relatives and said that the blood on the sheet was not from a maidenhead, but was ordinary menstrual blood. What a storm she unleashed, what clamour and protests arose between the two families! Even Domingas did not escape, for she was roundly cursed and accused of being a witch. The truth was, as she later found out from someone in the girl's family who was in on the secret, that the real sheet had been destroyed in a fire. The bride was afraid that the absence of proof on the day after the wedding would cause the break-up of her marriage, and so she arranged with one of her cousins to stain a different sheet with menstrual blood. It was also true, even if he did not remember it, that the groom had done the deed, there could be no doubt about that, as we shall hear.

When the news got out, one of the girl's aunts took the soiled sheet and went round to the groom's house brandishing it. "You rascal, shaming my niece in front of the whole village, and all over something you did yourself! Getting her a bad name! Curse you and your whole family, I'll split you in half. Speak up, you and your whore of a sister who's in there with you, if you come out here I'll break your head open. I want to hear you admit that my little girl was a virgin, I want to hear it right now, and from your very own lips. Speak up, you useless creature, we took you in when you were a poor soul with hardly a pair of drawers to your name, my little girl was run off her feet washing and cooking and I don't know what else, and this is the thanks we get! I'm not leaving till you own up. I'm a reasonable person, Joaquim, but who is that bloody old bitch Domingas to say the blood isn't such and such, and the girl had lost her whatever? It's a long time since Domingas lost hers, the old whore, the old witch."

Next came the girl's cousin, who had been hastily summoned as an eyewitness to the disputed event.

"Yes, Mr Joaquim, it was in my house that you had your way with my cousin, have you forgotten that already? Yes, you good-for-nothing, that's where it happened, and I'm alive to tell the tale, so just make your mind up to marry her. Are you trying to slip out of it? Don't you remember, the very night it happened, I heard the noise and went to have a look, and my cousin told me what had happened and showed me her clothes and everything, with you standing there, and you said it was no problem!"

The cousin was in a frenzy by this stage, one minute crouching down and beating the ground with the palms of her hands, the next untying the baby on her back and thrusting it to her breast to stop it crying, all the while making insulting gestures and challenging the groom's family to a fight. The whole neighbourhood was whispering and giggling, waiting to see the outcome of the affair, which was common enough, but not often conducted in such an open fashion.

Well, to return to the case of Arlete, which had really nothing to do with this old story, except insofar as it shows Domingas's skills and the scrapes they got her into:

"Dona Amélia, forgive me if I'm speaking out of turn, but in the girls' laundry-basket I found these soiled clothes which I think belong to Miss Arlete. I felt I had to tell you..."

"What about it, Josefa?"

"Ahem...Dona Amélia, to be quite frank, I think something must have gone on, Dona Amélia."

"Gone on, Josefa? What do you mean? What are you talking about?" asked Dona Amélia worriedly.

"Ahem, Dona Amélia, the thing is, I think, that is, I believe, she must have had relations, excuse the expression, Dona Amélia, because these bloodstains don't look like the usual monthlies. I showed them to Domingas and she..."

"What? Have you talked about this with Domingas?" cried Dona Amélia, throwing her hands in the air.

"Yes, Dona Amélia, I did it to make sure, because I would not like to misjudge any of your daughters; you've always been so kind to me and treated me as one of the family."

Domingas had confirmed in her symbolic Kimbundo that the blood on the garments was that of an innocent lamb; blood that had flowed for the first and only time; blood unlike any other.

"Not yet, Dona Amélia."

Arlete was so neat, shy, serene, untroubled and careful, the best-behaved of her brothers and sisters, that it had never occurred to Dona Amélia that she might give away her most prized possession before her wedding-night.

Arlete was the darkest-skinned of all her brothers and sisters, one could see she had black blood, she was a light-skinned mulatto, unlike her brothers and sisters, who could pass for white. Their great-grandmother was a black woman from Guinea-Bissau, who had married a man from Goa, and their grandmother was born in the Cape Verde Islands and had married a Portuguese. Dona Amélia was born in Mozambique and Sr Pinto, as it happened, in São Tomé. Arlete and some of the other children were born in Angola. So her special beauty was a sort of compendium of the old Portuguese Colonial Empire. She carried within her something of the charm of each of the colonies.

"Miss Arlete, do you need a doctor, or some medicine?"

"No, Josefa, as I told Mama, it's nothing..."

"Or do you need to bathe any particular part of your body? Have you a pain somewhere?"

"Why should I need to bathe any particular part, Josefa?" she asked in alarm, sitting up quickly and arranging a pillow behind her head.

"No special reason, but I'm a mother myself and I often cured my own daughters by getting them to sit in a bath with basil and angelica. But I see it's the time of the month, so maybe it would be better to avoid sitting in a hot bath."

"How do you know whether it's the time of the month or not, Josefa?"

"Well, I was sorting through the soiled clothes, and I..."

"What soiled clothes, where are they? Fetch the laundry-basket in the corner there and we'll have a look."

"I've already given it to the washerwoman, Miss."

"What insolence..."

Josefa put such pressure on Dona Amélia that she finally resolved to take her daughter to the doctor, but only after having a quiet word with him. She also sought the opinion of her friends in the Congregation of Mary. Dona Amélia was a pious Catholic, though some said it was for social reasons, to strengthen her husband's position. Presents of pigeons, chickens, baby goats and suckling pigs were sent to convents and churches, and there were always nuns and priests about the house. They were highly indignant about the whispers they heard and urged Amélia to take her daughter straight to the doctor. What God in his divine grace had given should only be offered up in the holy sacrament of matrimony.

Marajá had become famous since the championship, in which so many of his pupils had done him credit in both the ping-pong and the tennis. When he passed by, the youngsters practising soccer on makeshift pitches at Os Coqueiros and Kazuno would shout:

"There goes Marajá, isn't he smart!"

"No wonder the women like him!"

"Look at the way he walks, swinging his shoulders."

"He's a Don Juan!"

He was always well dressed, in second-hand clothes given by friends who were going off to university in Portugal. Sometimes they even sent him presents from there. He was a bit of a dandy. He would saunter along, showing off the athlete's muscles in his arms and legs. He had a well developed chest and lungs, thanks to his daily gymnastics. Neat, handsome, polite and well-mannered, he was really enchanting. After what had happened, he was surprised when three days passed with no news of his friend. Then he heard it being whispered in the dressing-rooms and corridors that Arlete was unwell, and shortly after, that she had been taken to the doctor with a suspected pregnancy!

"Arlete, my sweet, I see you're still not well, we'd better take you to the doctor tomorrow."

"But Mama, I feel better now, the pain's gone. I'll go to school in the afternoon. By the way, how is my beetle?"

"Never mind the beetle, it's safe enough. I don't like the look of you, you may have jaundice, it's better to be safe than sorry. You never know, an infection that is not caught in time can poison the whole system. If you don't want our own doctor to come and examine you at home, perhaps as it's a problem of the tummy or kidneys we could try some home remedies from the washerwoman, they say she's marvellous."

"What, Mama, me go to that old witch with her eggs? Ha, ha, ha," she laughed, "that's the last thing I need."

"Oh, don't say that, my sweet."

"But what is it you want, Mama? Don't you trust me? And don't you think that at seventeen, going on eighteen, I'm old enough to take care of my own business?"

"Well, you'll never be grown-up in my eyes, darling, you could be a grandmother and you'll still be a child to me.... You seem so changed nowadays... I'm your mother, and I know my own daughters."

"Very well, Mama, since you insist, I'll go to the doctor, but I'm not going anywhere near Domingas and her eggs."

When Sr Pinto learned what was going on, his first reaction was to send his daughter to Portugal. She need not bother to wait for her school examinations, she can take them next year. She can finish her last year in High School over there and enrol at the University. At least she would be near her grandparents and Chico and António (these were Arlete's older brothers, who were at university in Lisbon and Coimbra). His wife begged him not to take any rash decisions, until they found out if it was true, and who was responsible. "We'll do everything as discreetly as possible, to avoid any scandal. You know what happens with families in our position; not that we attach any importance to position; any little thing is blown up out of all proportion. I would not like us to lose the friendship and respect of our friends in the Church and in society, especially those in government circles."

So Arlete was taken to see the doctor and at the father's request he was sent a report:

MEDICAL REPORT

Virginity test on Arlete Pinto, seventeen years of age, born in Luanda, daughter of Jorge and Amélia Pinto. The results of the examination were as follows:

1 *A general physical examination revealed nothing unusual, no signs of bruising or recent violence.*
2 *A gynaecological examination revealed apparently recent tearing of the hymen, sustained in the last two or three days and probably caused by sexual intercourse.*
3 *The results of the examination demonstrate that the patient was recently deflowered.*

C.N. Lopes
Medical Gynaecologist
Luanda, 11 August 19...

Customs of the Town

ARLETE was seventeen years old, and already a woman, but she could not marry until she was eighteen and would remain a minor until the age of twenty-one. Moreover, the social and religious milieu in which her parents lived was full of prejudices. Until this moment, the Pintos had never thought, or even suspected, that their daughter was involved with any of the boys at the club or at the school, for none came regularly to the house. She was a quiet, sensible, home-loving girl, so much so that some thought her stuck-up and conceited, and she never paid any attention to boys, though they responded to her undoubted beauty—honey lips and eyes so tender—by hanging around outside her house, bowing and paying her compliments, but with the air of admirers who know they have no chance. In any case, the Pinto household was not open to just anyone: there were always expensive cars drawing up outside, with the monograms on the door of well-known figures in the Government, Army and Church, and the entrance to the house was guarded by two massive Alsatian dogs, who only had to snarl and bare their teeth to frighten off the most daring suitor.

In the days that followed the doctor's report, Sr Pinto's house was in turmoil. All the servants, especially Josefa and the washerwoman, were warned not to utter a single word outside about what had happened. Arlete, pressed to name the author of her misfortune, replied that no one had the right to ask. She respected her parents, to whom she owed her existence; she loved and cherished them, but this was a personal matter into which even a mother and father had no right to pry. It was nobody's business but hers. From conversations at school, she knew there were girls much younger than she who were involved with boys from the school, and nobody was scandalised. Why should she be any different?

Her parents could not believe what they were hearing from the lips of their child, who seemed utterly changed. They were her parents; she was still a minor; therefore in the eyes of the law and of the Church they were still responsible for her. They would use every means at their disposal to force Arlete to set their minds at rest by giving them the name of her seducer.

For the father, with or without the confession, one decision was irrevocable: Arlete was to sail for Portugal, far away, out of sight and out of reach of speculation and gossip. It was not only to prevent her from suffering, but also to protect the honour, prestige and dignity of the Pinto family; for there were those who might take advantage of the opportunity to besmirch the good name of such a well-known and respected family. There was a ship, the *Mouzinho*, at present making its way from West Africa; in the shipping agent's there was a notice that it had already left Beira and would be calling at Lourenço Marques, Cape Town, Lobito and Luanda. All the papers were got ready. Arlete was to be shipped aboard, and she did not even know!

The mother could not bear her daughter to leave without revealing her secret, and did everything she could to persuade her, but not one word did she manage to drag out of Arlete. Josefa advised Dona Amélia to consult a witch doctor. She began to look for one, and so did Domingas, but the cook said it was no good two people looking for a witch doctor in the same case. He himself knew a diviner who could solve the mystery. He asked Dona Amélia to give him a brand new white sheet which had never been slept on, a new coverlet, a bottle of sweet wine, another bottle of Port, a demijohn of white wine, money to buy a cockerel with a particular form of crest and money for the diviner. Josefa was also to get hold of one of the girl's shoes or slippers, a pair of her panties, clean or soiled, it did not matter, and some of her pubic hair.

"Oh, Joaquim," protested Josefa with a smile, "what a thing to ask, how on earth am I to get some of the young lady's pubic hair? If Dona Amélia could hear you she'd be shocked rigid and give up the whole idea!"

"That's all right, if the mistress wants it done, that's fine, if not, it's entirely up to her... you can easily get some pubic hair, just wait till the young mistress changes her panties and you'll see, even just one hair will do. Or wait till she gets out of bed, then you tell the maid not to make the bed or change the sheets without telling you, so you can take a peep and see if there's any hairs on the sheet."

"Good Lord, Joaquim, how is a person to know one kind of hair from another?"

"Come on, Josefa, don't try to kid me, all right? You telling me you can't get hold of pubic hair? You, a grown woman with daughters of your own, you talk like a fine lady from Portugal and you're trying to say you don't know the difference between hair from your head, hair from your armpit and hair from down below? If you folks want this done, get me what I say; if not, that's your problem."

So everything the cook had asked for was brought, but he had forgotten to mention a bottle of the wine that goes 'Pop!' when the cork is drawn. He used to know the name, but now he had to scratch his head trying to remember it.

"It's um...um...um... (staring at the sky for inspiration) ...It's that stuff, when you open it, it goes 'Pop!' and it sort of bubbles... fizzz..."

"Champagne?"

"That's it, exactly right! When the witch doctor is doing white man's business he has to call the white man's spirit into his head, and the spirit doesn't come if the black man has African food in his belly and has been swallowing African drink. He needs high-class wine so he can see into the white man's soul..."

Meanwhile, Dona Amélia remembered that her daughter had not been to confession for a long time. The family usually went to the Cathedral, so she went to speak to the priest there, who as a friend of the family already knew what had happened and how worried the mother was. He said he could see no way of inducing Arlete to confess the name, and even if she did, it was against the principles of the Church, and against his own principles, to reveal the secrets of the confessional. He advised Dona Amélia to be patient; everything would work out all right, she should not aggravate what was, after all, a common enough problem, and risk losing her daughter completely.

Joaquim, the cook, returned from his mission to the witch doctor bearing a hotch-potch of powders, herbs, potions and ointments, with strict instructions for their use. Josefa was informed of her role in the business, and Joaquim would look after the rest himself.

The next evening, mother and daughter were tenderly chatting. Dona Amélia tried her best to hide the sadness and anguish inside her, and began:

"My sweet, would you tell me if you were having some sort of relationship or love-affair with a boy, perhaps one of the boys from school...? Your father and I were very upset by the medical report..."

"Which medical report? What did it say?"

"The doctor sent it to us after your examination. It was not very reassuring... so we've been wondering what has been going on, and with whom?"

"Mama, you're not the only ones to notice something odd. I see Josefa has the impertinence to go poking around among my clothes, and I've overheard some of your conversations with your friends. It's not so terrible, it's natural, just like the girls in school told me. They said first you do this, then this happens..."

"Stop, stop, Arlete, you don't realise what you're saying," cried her mother, hiding her face in her hands and letting her head sink. She wept a little.

"Mama, first you ask me to tell you, then you start crying and saying I don't understand what I'm saying. One of these days I'll walk right out of this house and then you'll have no more problems..." As she said this, she rose to go out of the room. Dona Amélia was surprised by her daughter's reaction:

"Forgive me, darling, remember I'm a mother. Sit by me and tell me who the boy is."

"Mama, why must you know his name?"

"What a question! Don't you understand that you've committed a grave sin in the eyes of the Church, and a crime in the eyes of society? We need to know the boy's name in order to correct the mistake, if possible. The priests and nuns insist on that, it's the Church's teaching.''

"So you've brought them into it, have you, Mama? What if I won't tell? The priests and nuns never taught us anything about physical love, nor did you, and we were not exactly encouraged to ask the teachers in Moral Education. I simply conducted an experiment, just like I'm going to do with the white beetle in the school laboratory, to see if it's similar to the black beetle in its physical characteristics and behaviour…''

"Very well, Arlete, have it your own way, but please set my mind at rest, I feel I can hardly breathe. Who is the boy? You seem to know so much… I must confess I did not realise how much you had picked up in school or goodness knows where… Go on now, tell me who the boy is.''

"It's just an ordinary boy, Mama…''

Arlete got up to leave the room, crossing paths with Josefa who was coming to say she was leaving now. Seeing her mistress in tears, she inquired:

"Is anything wrong, Dona Amélia, can I fetch you a glass of water or a cup of tea, or should I fetch the doctor…?''

"Don't worry, Josefa, it's just a family matter. My head is spinning…'' and she began to sob. Sitting there with her hair in disorder, her head lolling on the back of the sofa and her arms dangling by her side, Dona Amélia was the picture of grief. After taking her a glass of water, Josefa made straight for Arlete's room. Sr Pinto and the rest of the family were at the cinema.

Arlete was lying on her back, staring at the ceiling, still dressed in her outdoor clothes and with her feet dangling over the end of the bed. Her arms were spread out as though she were being crucified, and she looked tired and pensive. Sunk in thought, she did not reply when Josefa knocked and asked if she could come in, nor did she grasp what Josefa was after when she asked what had happened between mother and daughter to make Dona Amélia cry.

Arlete was thinking about what might happen to Marajá. "He's black," she thought, "they only accept him as a coach, and even then, only up to a point. They might kill him, no, they couldn't because everyone would be on his side. All the young people who play sports, they all like him. Maybe they'll send him to prison, but I won't let them. I don't see why it's such a terrible sin, or crime. I only tried out what the other girls were talking about. It was a physical exercise; I didn't like it very much. Why all the fuss?" She was awake, but she suddenly felt as though Marajá was holding her round the waist and pressing down on her. "Not here in my parents' house, are you crazy? Don't Marajá, no, no!" She spoke these last words aloud, in Josefa's hearing.

Josefa then opened the door to go out, and as she did so Arlete realised she had been standing there for some time, waiting for the answer to her question. Frightened that she might have given something away, she sat up in bed, only to see Josefa wandering off, repeating her words, "Don't, Marajá, no, no." The servant was still wondering what was going on, since neither mother nor daughter would say what had happened. She decided it would be best to fetch the doctor, but as she stepped out of the gate she met Sr Pinto on his way back from the matinee with the younger children.

"Not gone home yet, Josefa?"

"Not yet, Sr Pinto, Dona Amélia is unwell. I think she's upset with Miss Arlete. But I asked them both, and neither will say a word."

On her way home to the native quarter, Josefa paid a visit to Domingas.

"Domingas, it's all quite clear now, I heard the mistress quarrelling with her daughter, then I found them both unwell, the mother crying and the daughter lying on her bed like a blooming oil-painting and talking in her sleep: 'Don't, Marajá, no, no!' "

"Marajá?" The old woman's eyes were like saucers. "You mean the porter up at the football club? You're joking, Josefa, come on now!"

"No, that's him, Bangu's nephew, that's right. I always had my suspicions about Arlete, she's a stuck-up, conceited little bitch."

"Yes, I know what you mean, I saw her one day wriggling her behind, and I thought, she's like a grasshopper about to lay eggs. She's no angel, that one. Any other boy I could understand, but Marajá, a black boy? and her the daughter of a rich white man who dines with lawyers, judges and governors. Oh, my God, Marajá, you've done it this time! They'll kill him, Josefa, you mark my words. Sleeping with the white man's daughter, and him just a servant, a nobody, a country bumpkin!"

"Shsh, Domingas, not a word to anyone. There's going to be big trouble tomorrow... I must say, Dona Amélia has had no luck with her children. First António and Chico, they're the ones who are at university in Portugal, they got mixed up with some girls and that's why they were packed off to Lisbon and Coimbra. Maria Madalena, she's twenty and they say she got herself in the family way over there in Porto, that's why Dona Amélia went over to Portugal last year. Let's see if the sixteen-year-old, Maria Ifigénia, gets herself into trouble at school. Jorginho's the father's favourite; he's only fourteen; he might turn out to be the quiet one... Listen, Domingas, don't you find Arlete a bit stuck-up?''

"She's a conceited, whorish little madam. Up there at the house she never has a glance or a kind word for anybody. So now she's gone and slept with a black boy, serves her right! Ha, ha, ha. But he must have been mad, somebody must have put a spell on him to make him sleep with such a lovely white girl, because she is lovely, I never saw such a beauty, she's like the painting of the guardian angel in the S. Paulo Church. Some angel now, Miss Arlete, eh? A fallen angel! Ha, ha, ha,'' and she clapped her hands as she said goodbye to Josefa who hurried crossly away.

The next morning, just as Arlete was leaving for school, she was detained by her father, who wanted a serious talk.

"Arlete, your mother and I are not prepared to suffer heart-break and make ourselves ill over something you can easily solve. I want the name of this ordinary boy you mentioned.''

"Papa, I cannot understand why everyone is so anxious to know his name, and I must say I never expected to have to discuss these things with my father.''

"Who else, since you refuse to confide in your mother? We need to take steps...''

"What steps, Papa?''

Silence from the father, who gazed wrathfully at his child's wide eyes and trembling lips.

"The name, Arlete!''

"Very well. You want the name, is that right?'' Beside herself with anger, in a changed voice she said: "It's Marajá.''

Sr Pinto was glued to the sitting-room carpet. He saw stars before his eyes and reaching behind him felt for the edge of the sofa, onto which he collapsed.

Arlete remained only a short time in her bedroom; then she went to the club to tell Marajá everything and warn him what might happen. She advised him to go to the Island, to the home of Sr Felix and Dona Laura, a childless couple who were very fond of him. For herself, she did not know the fate that awaited her, but from her mother's behaviour she sensed that something strange was being planned. Her father was in the habit of shipping his children off to Portugal whenever anything went wrong. She wouldn't accept that. She wanted to finish her last year of school in Luanda. She felt sorry for Marajá, who was the real victim. "Perhaps I should confide in Gioconda and Maria Celeste, two girls at school who are older and have more experience in these affairs of the heart; everyone gossips about them at break."

Sr Pinto went to the police to charge Marajá with taking advantage of his daughter during a sports lesson and forcing her to participate in a sexual act under threat of death if she told her parents.

"Sr Pinto, wouldn't it be better if we heard the whole story from your daughter and this boy before taking it any further?" asked the head of criminal investigations.

"No need. The girl is under age, seventeen years old, and I have the medical report here. All you have to do is arrest him and send him straight to prison, but make sure you handcuff him and give him a good going-over with a rhino-whip. After the trial I'll have a word with some officer friends and see he's banished for a good long stretch to Forte Roçadas..."

"But Sr Pinto, you said your daughter was sailing tomorrow or the day after for Portugal. In that case the trial cannot go ahead as you wish..."

"We lay the facts before the court, my daughter sails, that

rascal goes to prison, and I'm sure we can rely on..."

"Special detention... I take your point. But I don't see how it can be done..."

Both the police and court officials went to find the criminal, armed with warrants for his arrest. Marajá had taken refuge in Sr Felix's house, giving him a confused account of events, though making it clear that the police and the courts were after him. Sr Felix, who was also one of the directors of the soccer club, was very fond of the boy and had helped him a good deal: it was thanks to him that Marajá had finished his primary education and was now at a private secondary school. Felix's wife, Dona Laura, was a quarrelsome lady with a tongue like a viper. She was very proud of being one-hundred-percent Portuguese, and had some reservations about the Pintos, especially Dona Amélia. She had long ago stopped visiting their house, and would criticise her husband harshly for hanging around the other couple:

"For all I know, you're borrowing money from him, or he's taking you to gambling dens, or worse. All I get from you is, 'I was up at Pinto's house', or 'I was discussing some problems about the club with Pinto'. What a stupid husband I have, to go crawling to a man like that. Sometimes I wonder if it isn't old Amélia you're after," she would say with an ironic laugh. "Hypocritical bitch, she spends half her time kissing the feet of the nuns and priests, and the other half casting spells with her witch of a servant... don't tell me you're pretending to be friends with Pinto to get hold of his hen, for that's what she is, a wrinkled old hen..."

"Do be quiet, Laura, you seem to be beside yourself today... I was with Pinto, as a matter of fact, and he told me what happened between his daughter and Marajá; a very serious business. God alone knows what the truth of the matter is, but Marajá could find himself facing a jail sentence. It's a pity…"

"Marajá in jail? Never! I'll see Amélia in jail first, and her whore of a daughter. Jail, Marajá? Over my dead body! Marajá, come quickly and tell us what you did to Queen Amélia's daughter. Speak up, don't be afraid."

"I didn't do anything, it's a lie."

"You must at least have tried something. Which one was it, anyway, Madalena, Efigénia or Arlete?"

"It was Arlete, Dona Laura."

"Well, you showed good taste, she's the prettiest and the best-educated. So they're complaining she's under age? Who are they trying to fool? She has hips and breasts on her that are crying out for a man! Well, it's one in the eye for her holier-than-thou mother, all day long she's with the priests and nuns, then at night with the witch doctors her servants bring. After all his good work at the championships, this is Marajá's reward, lies and slander. I bet it was her that egged you on, wasn't it? From now on you call me godmother, and Felix is godfather, no more Dona Laura and Sr Felix, okay?"

Turning to her husband she added:

"Off you go and tell Pinto to use his head and not go making trouble for your godson. And tell Dona Amélia, the so-called grieving mother, she'd better lock up her daughters in the convent at Mafra, or even better in the convent unmasked, if she remembers her Victor Hugo. And tell that chicken Pinto he should act like a rooster and keep an eye on his daughters and his hen. Tell him to take care of Amélia himself, and not expect you to do the job for him."

"Laura, be quiet."

"I will not be quiet."

A Busy Night

IT WAS EARLY morning, and dawn was rising over Luanda. A slight mist hung in the air, and Sr. Pinto could hardly see the road as he walked up to St. Michael's Fort and trained his binoculars on the islands of Mussulo, Xicala and O Cabo, where the giant ship was sailing in majestically, all her lights ablaze.

It was the *Mouzinho*, considered at that time a luxury liner. Sr. Pinto took a long look, for it was his favourite ship. She would dock this morning, then set off again at 18.00 hours that same day for Funchal, on the island of Madeira, and then Lisbon. She advanced slowly amid the spray flung up by her prow. Two small motor-launches set off to meet her from the pier, near where the Post Office and Naval Head-quarters are now, in Rua Marginal. "The first one must be the doctor, and the second from the shipping company or the port authorities," thought Pinto. He swung his binoculars round and stared at the massive, gloomy bulk of the prison, which contrasted sharply with the luxury liner in which Arlete was to be banished to Portugal. The prison was a pigsty, stinking of mould and the breath of many men condemned to death inside: that's where Marajá was bound, Bangu's nephew, the well-known Don Juan and dandy. Who would have thought that the man who had received so many kisses from pretty girls on the day of the championship would end up in a dungeon!

It was 6.47 a.m. Sr Pinto went home content, to wake up his daughter. When she appeared in the sitting-room, her mother and father explained matters to her with their usual tact: she was to sail on the *Mouzinho* that day. "We could not say anything before, we were waiting for a medical report. Thanks to you, your mother has some trouble with her nerves, which has given rise to a heart condition. You're to go to Portugal to keep her company. You'll be back in a month..."

"Mama, I'm sorry, but I'm not going to Portugal. I happen to know that your health is not the real reason. They're going to arrest Marajá, aren't they, Papa? Well, let me tell you, that would be very wrong, for if anyone was to blame it was me. If you force me to go on that ship, I'll take my own life, I'll throw myself overboard."

"Arlete, have you no pity for your sick mother?"

"I have, Papa, but that is not the issue at the moment."

"Don't you love us? Think of your ailing mother, who loves you so much."

"Mama, if you need to be accompanied, in Portugal you have my brothers Chico and António and my sister Madalena; what's to stop them interrupting their studies, if it was all right for me to do so? And apart from them, there are all the aunts and uncles on your side and Papa's."

"Once and for all, are you going?"

"Papa, I've never refused to do anything you've asked, even that time in Johannesburg, when you took all the others to a party at the home of the Burgomeister, Sr Wagner, who was a friend of yours from Lourenço Marques; I did as I was told. I stayed behind in the hotel-room crying. The servants told me Sr Wagner asked you to leave me behind because I had darker skin than the others, and some of the important guests would not like to see a coloured person at the table..."

"Hush, Arlete, whatever gave you such an idea, and about something which happened so long ago? You know you're our favourite, how could those servants make up such a story? You'll break your papa's heart," wailed Dona Amélia, putting her hands over her ears and beginning to sob.

Sr Pinto went on board the ship, to check on the sailing-time and to inspect the cabin which his wife and daughter were to occupy. He ran into an old friend of his, a Brazilian named Dr Camargo, who was a philosopher, sociologist and ethnographer, as well as teaching law at one of the Brazilian universities. They greeted each other with hearty backslapping.

"Fancy meeting you here, Camargo."

"Well, well, Pinto, haven't seen you for years. I'm on my way to Portugal and from there back to Rio. I've been staying with friends in Lourenço Marques... but you look very anxious and depressed, is business not going so well? Sit down for a minute..." They sat down at one of the tables in the first class bar, and Pinto told his friend his troubles.

"Oh, Pinto, I'm afraid you've been very foolish. Honestly, the things you parents find to worry about! You're all worked up because your daughter isn't a virgin at seventeen? My goodness, for all you know, the hymen may have gone because of all the excitement of this war against the Germans! The girl may not even have noticed. These are troubled times we live in; don't concern yourself any more about it."

"No, I took her to the doctor..."

"Proves nothing. Look, you should be in Brazil, there you would think the girls were born without hymens, and you're worried about a seventeen-year-old. Honestly, Pinto, you're behind the times. And don't mention nuns and monks, because some of them lost their most precious possession even before they became novices, and now they want to make a martyr of your daughter, isn't that so? You're still living in the last century, in our grandparents' time. Or is it perhaps the thought of losing the Church business that bothers you, you fear they may excommunicate your livestock and produce because of your daughter's lapse?"

"It's nothing to do with that, Camargo. What really worries me is that it was with a black, one of the servants from the club, who will never amount to anything, and they weren't even in love."

"Don't talk rubbish, Pinto, everyone has some chance of amounting to something. I gave a lecture only a fortnight ago on the racial question. Which daughter was it anyway?"

"You know, the one who..."

"About whom there was that painful incident in Johannesburg?"

"Yes."

"Well, there you are, then. Your daughter's feelings for the black boy are entirely natural. There has been some research recently into the question of the mingling of races in different parts of the world, and they have found families which had gone completely white reverting to black, and vice versa. You cannot ignore heredity. I could give you thousands of well-documented cases. Your daughter falls in love with this black boy and she has a child, which might look just like me; that is, I look white, but my great-grandfather was a black slave from Africa, so my children, or my grand-children, or great-grand-children may very well be born black. Did you know that the greatest mathematician ever known was from the ancient University of Egypt, so he certainly wasn't white. Don't give the matter another thought...."

Returning home, Sr Pinto found a large number of visitors who had come to console Dona Amélia, persuade Arlete to take the trip "to keep Mama company", and say goodbye to both. Arlete, unmoved by all the good advice, managed to whisper to a friend that if she sailed it would be the death of her, for she would throw herself into the sea, like Mariana in the Portuguese novel *Amor de Perdição,* or *She Died for Love*, though in her case it was not for love, since all she had been doing with Marajá was practising a new sport.

Marajá was reassured by his godmother Laura's words, and thought that by now the storm would have abated, so that afternoon he set off around four o'clock for the tennis courts at the club, in Os Coqueiros, looking very handsome in his shorts, gym shoes, white socks and sports shirt, and carrying his racquet and a box of tennis balls. It was one of those long, pleasant afternoons, not too hot. Marajá had been training at courts belonging to a friend of Sr Felix on the Island, for ever since the fatal day he had not gone back to work at the club nor shown his face in public.

At the entrance to the club there were some girls who knew him. "Hello, Marajá," they called, "haven't seen you for ages. Give you a game?" But no sooner was he inside than he was accosted by a policeman, who showed him the warrant for his arrest and asked Marajá to accompany him. The girls were astonished and crowded round the police vehicle, trying to find out what was going on.

"Gioconda," said Marajá to one of them, "can you come here a moment? Please take this racquet and tennis balls to Sr Felix and tell him I've been arrested."

"You're not allowed to say that, no talking," the police man ordered peremptorily. "What did you say? Arrested?" cried Gioconda, attracting the attention of all those inside. A curious crowd began to gather, but the police van was already pulling away.

Slowly, languidly, the sun began to sink into the sea. It was like a huge ball of fire, crimson as blood, the centre of a circle of light-beams that played over the calm, undulating surface of the waves, forming a scene of great beauty. As though to complete the picture, flights of sea birds swooped inside the charmed circle of sunbeams in search of a calm resting-place for the night. Arlete was sitting all alone by St Michael's Fort, on a stone on which hundreds before her had sat down to rest. She awoke from a long reverie and, rising from her seat, walked round to the other side of the Fort where the ground was higher.

"The world is a beautiful place," she thought to herself, watching the circles of the dying sun being swallowed by the sea, and thinking that she would be swallowed in the same way if they forced her to go on the ship. She had run out of the house two hours earlier, fleeing from the insistent coaxing of friends who wanted her to sail. If she had left a few seconds later, at the ice-cream parlour her path would have crossed that of Marajá in the police van, on his way to the distant dungeons of the main prison. Now she lifted her gaze from the islands of Samba, Cabeleira and Xicala and turned it towards the *Mouzinho* from whose side the smaller launches and tugs were departing. Though she did not know it, her father that morning had watched the ship's arrival from the very same spot at which she now stood watching its departure, with neither herself nor her mother on board.

Boo...oom, Boo...oom... went the ship's horn, bidding farewell to Luanda and summoning those passengers who had still not come aboard...Boo...oom, Boo...oom, it sounded again. Arlete trembled, her stomach churned and she felt nervous and confused; warm tears ran down her cheeks, leaving a salty taste on her lips, and down to her chest, trickling on to the tips of her breasts, which Marajá had never even touched. She brought out a handkerchief with which she dried her tears and blew her nose. The thought crossed her mind of throwing herself off the Fort; then she would be no trouble to anyone and would not have to put up with the hail of recriminations at home. "Then they'll be the ones to weep, not me."

"Forget this wild idea," said a strange voice. And looking round, she saw plants and bushes and the crimson leaves of acacia inviting her to abandon her gloomy thoughts. From the barracks of the First Native Company—it was in the part of the city now called "the barracks", or "the Comandante Gika School", and this was in the days when the city was small, with few cars or noisy factories to pollute the environment—came the echo of the bugles and drums of the changing of the guard at General Military Headquarters, Government House, the Governor's Residence, the National Treasury and the prison.

Arlete heard the call "Present Arms!" from General Military Headquarters, then again as the guard reached Government House, "Preseeent Arms!" She began to listen, distracted for a moment from her problems, as a third "Preseeent Arms!" was heard, indicating the arrival of the new guard at the Governor's Residence. There was a roll of drums, accompanied by bugle-calls, one indicating that the flag was being hoisted.

The ceremony of the changing of the guard was a simple one, but it was exciting, full of colour and interest. The black soldiers marched with thrust-out chests, grim faces and fearsome, shining eyes. They had haversacks on their backs and rifles on their shoulders with bayonets gleaming on the ends. They wore crimson berets with the numeral 1 on the front to indicate First Native Company, and were barefoot, though wearing gaiters with grey and brown bindings. Their tunics and shorts were khaki with shiny gold buttons. The changing of the guard was a daily spectacle for passers-by, especially for the children who ran alongside on both sides of the road and accompanied the tramp, tramp, tramp of the soldiers' bare feet, thudding on the ground like hobnailed boots. Once they got to Government House there was a picturesque ceremony, full of complicated maneouvres, which the native soldiers, most of them illiterate, executed with iron discipline. Black and white alike stopped to watch, and every single car, even down to the Governor General's vehicle, with its flag on the front, stopped to let the native troops pass. This was the only time the native was treated with respect, and even awe, by everyone. All the barracks, government buildings and arsenals were guarded by blacks. Of course, they were blacks who could be trusted, like Marajá. Yet now here was Marajá being packed off to jail in defiance of all legal safeguards, which only showed that for Marajá and others like him, crime and punishment were dictated by the colour of their skin.

It was growing dark, but the prison could still be glimpsed. "That's where my father swore he'd have Marajá locked up," thought Arlete. "It's late, I'd better go back down."

Walking down Condemned Man's Alley, she saw Captain Paias going past with his wife and children.

"I know that girl from somewhere," his wife remarked.

"Me too," the captain agreed.

Marajá had been taken from the tennis club to the police station, and from there straight to the prison, which was very unusual. As he was being taken into the jail, he crossed paths with the daughters of Captain Sena, the prison governor. They recognised him:

"Aren't you Marajá?"

"Yes, Miss Zeta."

The girls went to have a word with their father, who was already in the car, asking him to ensure that Marajá was treated properly, since he had not stolen anything, nor been in a fight, nor murdered anybody. "He's a friend of ours from the tennis club."

"Hush, girls, I'll see about it when we get back, let's go now. These people have never done anything wrong, then later you find they're the world's biggest rascals."

"Papa, that's a terrible thing to say, he's the nicest and most respectful black boy we've ever known, so well-mannered, and he wouldn't hurt a fly."

"Or even an ant," her sister added.

By the time the ship's horn sounded, Marajá was being locked up in the communal cell, but first he asked the warder, a black soldier with a grim expression, if he could go the toilet.

"What? Come on, get in quick, any shitting you have to do you can do in there. At this time of night, shitting is done in the cell. He's hardly in and he wants out again, did you ever hear the like? Don't try and get funny with me, you thief. Hey, you men in there, show this rat the throne!'' (This is what they called the slop-pail.) ''Don't try to be smart in here, you may be a big shot in the slums you come from, but here all it gets you is a beating or a kick in the arse or the balls, geddit? Here it's Yessir, Yessir, from morning till night, and you say it properly, none of the Yessah. In the morning, the first thing you do is empty the slop-pail. You hear me in there?''

''Yeah, sure, we know...''

''Listen, I recognise that boy,'' said one of the prisoners, ''he coaches girls up at the club.'' The guard was closing the door, its heavy, black, iron bars smeared with foul-smelling grease from the hands of countless unwashed prisoners handling saucepans and plates. He misunderstood what had been said, and shouted furiously at Marajá:

''Wha-a-a-t? So that's what you've been up to, coaching girls? Get those trousers down and I'll soon see to it you don't do it again! You dirty little devil, I've had all sorts in here, robbers, murderers, drug-pushers, all I needed was somebody who's been coaching girls.''

''But Corporal, it's tennis, you know, he's been teaching girls to play tennis.''

''Aahah!'' muttered the jailer, growing calmer before the astonished gaze of Marajá, who was clinging tightly to his trousers.

It was busy night for everyone. Dona Amélia did not board the ship. As for Arlete, all the efforts of her father and friends to find her proved vain. They went to the jetty, expecting to find her there. There was the possibility of suicide, according to the confession of the friend to whom Arlete had whispered her intentions. Gioconda and some friends formed two groups, one to search for Arlete, the other to knock at the doors of all their most influential contacts, to urge them to persuade Sr Pinto to adopt some other measure. They also wanted Marajá released that very night, partly out of affection for Arlete, but also because of Marajá's own reputation in the world of sport. They saw the Military Commander, the Chief of Staff, the Chief of Police, the President of the Town Council, the High Court Judge, the daughter of the Governor-General, the daughter of Brandão de Melo, eminent lawyers and everyone who frequented the tennis club or sent their children there.

These valiant attempts by the girls to obtain the release of their tennis and ping-pong coach were highly significant, but we must not forget Bangu, who approached Sr Pinto and other prominent club members. Sr Felix knew no rest that night, to say nothing of his wife, who roundly cursed Dona Amélia, and warned her husband not to come home without Marajá, otherwise she'd pluck out every last one of that chicken Pinto's feathers.

"All we ever heard from you," she complained bitterly, "was 'I was with Pinto', or 'I was up at Pinto's place', yet he never once told you what was going on with our godson, the foul hypocrite. He's a cheat and a coward, just like yourself. So now people are to be arrested in the street, without even knowing what for? I'll get my own back on that whited sepulchre Amélia, she should lock up her daughters in a convent. Do you think a black boy like Marajá, so clever and well-mannered, would have the nerve to lay a finger on the daughter of Sr Pinto who's such a big shot around here? Knowing Pinto, you believe a story like that? For all we know, some white boy is responsible and our poor black friend is being made to take the blame. Up you get and bring Marajá back with you. Your friend Pinto and Holy Mother Amélia had better let him go. If not, I'll create an almighty scandal. There's not a soul believes their slanders.''

Felix did not answer, but lay down on the bed, too tired from running around to do more than take off his shoes. His wife was not deterred:

"Felix, get up. I want Marajá back. You can't go to sleep, on your feet and go after the boy.'' Dona Laura began to pull and tug at her husband's feet, making such a fuss that he ended up by putting on his shoes and going out.

"That's it. And feel free to sleep with Amélia or wherever you want. What sort of man are you, boasting about your friendship with Pinto and yet you can't get the boy released…''

So a very unusual situation existed, where there was a conflict between black and white and the whites were on the black person's side, especially considering Marajá's social position. The usual thing in these disputes was for everyone to line up behind his race, with no idea who was in the right.

The girls' activities caused such an impression among the boys at school that even those who were previously neutral or indifferent joined the cause, in a sporting spirit which gave rise to slogans like this, dreamed up in the break:

A la bim, a la bom, a la bim bom ba,
Marajá, Marajá, rah, rah, rah.

Who do we want?
Marajá!
When do we want him?
Now!

The authorities grew alarmed, as what had seemed a routine case turned into a militant political cause that might be used for who knows what ends. Policemen lurking around the

112

school were mocked: ''Are you there, Marajá?'' a group of students would call out, with one eye on the police. Alert and suspicious, the flatfoot would scowl furiously.

The next day, Tuesday, around six in the evening, Marajá was bailed out of prison by his godfather Felix and a rich businessman.

After the excitement had died down a little, the young people who had mobilised in the cause thought it a pity to lose the awareness that had been aroused in certain members of the white élite, so they planned a new offensive. There was to be no trial, and instead Arlete was to be persuaded to marry her lover. (These young people were active, but they did not always stop to analyse problems carefully.)

Up till now it had been easy, but they could not see how to overcome the huge barriers between Arlete, the daughter of rich, white, upper-class parents, who moved in high circles and was educated and refined, and Marajá, a black caretaker at a soccer club, with no professional qualifications and descended from poor peasants who went around in breech-clouts. He had little education and was not even from the native quarter of the city, which was unknown to him, since he had been raised in the soccer club, in the downtown, European area of the city. Yet he could not be said to truly belong to that environment, being only a tennis and ping-pong coach. Really he was a country boy, who did not belong to either the black or the European quarters of the city.

It went without saying that Arlete's parents would probably prefer to see her dead than committing such a crime, for not only was it contrary to their social position, it would be seen as a betrayal of her race, causing it to degenerate rather than improve.

At that time it was not very common for black men to marry

white women. There were just one or two cases of black men who lived in Portugal and married white wives whom they would bring over for a holiday. Nor were there many examples of white men married to black or mixed-race women, and those there were, naming no names, suffered discrimination in their social and professional life. Where a black man did marry a white woman, it was unlikely to be a happy, successful marriage, for wherever they went in Angola, and no matter what the man's social position, he would be the butt of direct insults from the whites and perhaps more subtle mockery from his fellow-blacks, to say nothing of the black mothers and sisters who would take every opportunity to wound and criticise in coarse terms the relative who brought them a white girl-friend or wife—this was in the old days.

However, when youth is united and determined to carry out a plan, no power on earth can resist it. The young people went round testing opinion, trying to provoke their parents by hinting that Arlete had made up her mind to marry Marajá, come what might, because her parents had caused her so much misery, and she was so upset with them, that the only way she could get her own back was to marry a black. Arlete knew nothing of these tales that were being put about by her friends, but whispered rumours reached her parents, and then one day an old friend, a well-known businessman, told them in so many words what was being said.

Sr Pinto and Dona Amélia were scandalised and thought that the young people and the few adults who had got mixed up in the affair were absolutely crazy. ''Never will I consent to such a crime, while there's blood in my veins,'' Pinto proudly swore, crossing himself and beating his heart with his closed fist...

The young people received discouraging advice from all sides, parents claiming that with more experience in these matters, they could not encourage a marriage which they foresaw would be unhappy.

Dona Laura heard the rumours which were beginning to circulate about her godson's marriage to Arlete. Sr Felix confirmed the rumour, but he thought it was impossible it should ever happen, and he refused to bring the subject up with Pinto, who was annoyed with him for sheltering Marajá. True or false, Dona Laura was delighted and began to make plans to get her godson ready for the magnificent ceremony, which would be attended by all the top people in the colony, considering the social position of the bride's father. It was wonderful news! Radiant with joy, Dona Laura called out to a neighbour stationed by her window:

"Dona Sofia, have you got a moment?"

"Yes, Dona Laura, what is it?"

"Come over, I'll only keep you a second."

Dona Sofia came running down the stairs, her little, thin legs encased in high boots. She was the town's number one gossip, and did not want to miss this special broadcast.

"Did you hear that my godson is to marry Sr Pinto's daughter?"

"You don't say!"

"I most certainly do say, you can ask my husband. Well Dona Sofia, isn't it wonderful?"

"Yes, congratulations, Dona Laura."

"Oh, it's a bit early for that, but..."

Marajá, who went out to exercise early every morning on the beach near the house, had just come strolling in and noticed the two ladies. Round his neck was a white towel with red and blue stripes, on his head a blue sports-cap, and he wore a nice pair of swimming trunks.

"Here comes my godson. He hasn't said a word; he's a rascal, but he must know what's going on. Don't you find him handsome, Dona Sofia?"

"Of course I do. He's a fine figure of a man, so good-looking. No wonder the girls are mad about him, and then there's something about him, you couldn't say what colour he is, he doesn't look black, nor mixed-raced, nor white, I've never seen anyone like him. The girls are quite right to find him attractive, I don't blame Saint Amélia's daughter." (They broke into peals of laughter at their own loose talk, which is very African, but at the same time typical of these Lisbon ladies in the posh parts of town.) "I never saw a black with such lovely, smooth feet."

Marajá smiled complacently.

"Run along and change, then come back in and I'll give you some good news."

"Do I have to go back to jail, godmother?"

"Jail my foot, this time the captive is Pinto's daughter."

"And she couldn't ask for a handsomer jailer, my boy; it's just a pity you're black," was Dona Sofia's parting shot.

Josefa's Lesson

THE BUZZINGS about Arlete marrying Marajá sped about, rose in volume and at last grew troublesome to Sr. Pinto's household. For their part, the young supporters never let up in their pressing and preparing for the match. Arlete, challenged by her parents to say how she felt about these rumours, declared she knew nothing about them, but perhaps destiny called her to accept what her friends and companions said...

"I hope destiny won't make you bring disgrace on the family or my good name, otherwise I'll do something we'll all be sorry for, do you hear me, Arlete?" her father threatened.

Josefa, attentive to all the gossip and scandal that whirled round her employers' home, fell into a melancholy musing. This followed several chats with Domingas, the old washerwoman who did the divining with eggs. So off Josefa went to the linen room and sat down on the bench she usually stood on to get linen out of the cupboards. Elbows on the table, she rested her head on her hands and thought with great concentration, every now and then nodding her head and saying to herself: "Well, well, well." Then she began:

"But how on earth can Miss Arlete, born and bred in this country and knowing the way blacks live, want to marry a black boy? She must be bewitched. She's blind, poor thing. When you get a black man marrying a white woman, the woman always ends up going back to Portugal, when she's not kidnapped or persuaded not to go through with it by whites annoyed at seeing one of their own going off with a black, nothing but a servant. So this Marajá, out of vanity or cheek, wants to show off his white lady to his parents, does he? Just picture it! The parents are dirt poor, they live out in the bush in a mud hut, you have to get down on your knees to crawl in. Or if they're here in the native quarter it's a lath-and-plaster shack with a corrugated iron roof, one kitchen for everybody, pigs, chickens and a goat tied to a stake, all in the same room, the table's a wooden crate, you sit on the ground or on a stone—that's where Marajá is going to show off his lovely white wife! Black women living in sin with white men, I've known plenty of cases. But a church wedding? That's different. Can it be that Arlete just wants to take revenge on her parents, with no thought for her own future? This Gioconda and her other school-friends who are encouraging Arlete, you don't see them going with blacks. A white woman kissing a black from the bush—unless you're talking about white trash—it's a disgrace! I'm black myself, but I'm not proud of it! I've made up my mind, I'm going to help Dona Amélia. I mean, if the boy was one of those blacks from São Tomé, or if it was one of those black sailors hoodwinking a white girl in Portugal, her not knowing about Africa and him letting on they might find gold or diamonds, I could understand, or him kidding her his parents were kings over here, okay. But Miss Arlete, who knows all about blacks, how could she ever get involved in this? Wouldn't marry a black myself, much less one from the bush. Oh, God, Miss Arlete, I can just see you among those saucy niggers out in the village. Off you go to meet your parents-in-law. The mother-in-law starts giving orders, 'cos that's what it's like out there: go and fetch water from the river, and off you go with a gourd or a jug on your head. Very nice for a white girl! Now get the firewood, and there goes Miss Arlete with a machete in her hand, and all the tattered bush children and old women trotting along beside her... off into the thickets to cut branches and bring them back on her head. Oh, Lord, Miss Arlete, now grind me some millet or some manioc flour, and the girl asks her, Mother, how do you work the mortar and pestle?... Oh, Miss Arlete. And that swinish old woman gets angry and snorts, what sort of daughter-in-law is this, Marajá, she's good for nothing...Ay, ay, ay, Miss Arlete. Then up comes the father with just a little cloth over his privates, no shirt, swaggering like his son, and he calls out Eeh, daughter-in-law Dilete, (he can't get his tongue around Arlete, the dirty old dog, no teeth and always drunk), bring me a coal from the fire to light up a pipe of hemp... Ay, Blessed Virgin... What do you say to this, Miss Arlete? The girl, out of sheer politeness and respect, and because she loves a common black, a bushman, takes it all, and off she goes to the fire in the cooking-place—for you can hardly call it a kitchen, all out in the open air. She brings him an ember and says: Papa, here's your light... So, Miss Arlete, how do you like your black daddy?''

Tired of sitting in the same position, Josefa crossed her legs under the table, leaned her chin on one hand and laid the other on the table:

''And here's Marajá's mother, his aunts and other relatives, for these people have no shame, all arriving as cheeky as you like at Dona Amélia's house. Come in from the bush to meet the bride's parents. Down they sit at the table, they can't eat with a fork, not even with a spoon, just grab fish, meat or rice with their fingers: there goes the gravy running down their fingers onto the snow-white cloth, food onto the carpet. They shout for more wine, then start up their dances, just like in the bush, vulgar dances, in this house full of beautiful carpets and mirrors. That fellow's never seen a mirror, he bangs into it and smashes it to pieces...Ay, Miss Arlete, is this the sort of people you're going to bring to Dona Amélia's house, where once governors, doctors, bishops and really grand company used to come? Are we now to fall so low, that I must put up with this rabble, just because you take a fancy to Marajá, a builder's labourer with his barrow full of cement and lime? No, no, I won't put up with it, and Dona Amélia doesn't deserve this from her favourite daughter. If only Marajá would die, uppity nigger. The bush blacks around here are too big for their boots, not like José Maquita's people. He was a black, with big lips, but lived in Portugal ever since he was a child. He came back with a pretty white wife, and when he took her out to meet his parents in the bush the old people ran off, saying their son had brought them a mermaid. But in Marajá's region they're very uppity, I'd set fire to the lot of them... They've no fear or respect for the white man, that's why white people don't like them, wherever they go they bring trouble for everyone.

"Marajá, you've cast a spell on the white girl. My life was nicely arranged, now it's all spoiled thanks to you... A good job and a good life; I gave the orders in this house. Now the masters will go off to Portugal and I'll be back where I started... Damn you, Marajá, black trash. But you'll pay for this, I'm going to bury a red cockerel alive and you'll die! If you escape that, I'll go to Saint Anna's Church, or Our Lady of Muxima, because you've no right to ruin other people's lives, Marajá..."

By now the laundry list lay on the table in front of Josefa soaked with tears, the ink running and completely illegible. She wiped her eyes and blew her nose on a handkerchief, just like a lady, her eyes puffy from weeping.

(Note 'like a lady', because of course the term 'lady' could really be applied only to a white. No black servant would ever consider another black or mulatto a 'lady', and if much later they had to use the word about a woman who wasn't white, they did so reluctantly and because it was beaten into them. Influence of the white mentality.)

The housekeeper was awakened from her trance by the voice of Dona Amélia, who was very depressed, almost to the point of a nervous breakdown, over the problem of her daughter and the failure of the proposed trip on the *Mouzinho*. She decided to consult Josefa, amid sobs:

"Josefa, I don't know what is to become of me. The devil has come into this house. Arlete must be mad to even think of marrying that boy. What a fate! Is there no way your people can find me a cure for her?"

"I'm sick to death myself, Madam, thinking about all this, but don't worry, I'll fix it, I'll have another word with old Joaquim, the cook."

Once told of the situation, Joaquim went off to consult the witch doctor again. Two days later, he asked Josefa if it was just to change the girl's mind, or kill the boy by a spell.

"Listen, Joaquim, nothing complicated, all the mistress wants is for her daughter not to marry the damned boy. Do whatever is most convenient, but quickly, because the mistress is going funny in the head."

"To tell the truth, it's not that easy. I'm no witch doctor, I'm only passing on what he told me. The thing is, if it's to kill the boy, that's a big problem and it takes months. If it's to make the girl change her mind, that's quite difficult as well, but it's quicker. If it's to kill the boy, the mistress must stop going to church every morning while the witch doctor is working on it. If it's to change the girl's mind, the girl must not go to church either for nine days. She must ask the boy to massage her body or hand, or else the mother has to ask the boy to the house and speak to him..."

"What, Joaquim? The boy's to come here to the house to speak to Dona Amélia?"

"Of course! What did you expect?"

"But is all this really necessary?"

"Look, if you don't like it, that's your problem. If you prefer, get the mistress to go to the Church of Saint Anna in Caxito or Saint Anthony's in Kifangondo," said the old man angrily.

"Okay, I'll pass it on to the mistress and tell you what she says..."

"Yes, and tell her you can't mix the two things at the same time, the church and the witch doctor, except in very unusual cases. Take my uncle, for example, he's dead now, but he was a catechist in the church, and then I had another uncle, my mother's brother. He's dead too, he was a witch doctor. You should have heard them arguing, they got really angry, but in really serious cases they would work together, they both went to church and to the *quimbanda* where the witch doctor works, oh, I nearly forgot, Josefa, the mistress has to go there herself later on. She has to take a pair of the girl's panties and a shoe or a sock belonging to the boy."

"Does she really have to, Joaquim?"

"Listen, I'll have you know plenty of ladies go there, really high-up people."

Dona Amélia, put in the picture by her housekeeper, sat silent for a while, staring at the ceiling. Then she sighed, gestured and moaned:

"This is a heavy cross to bear."

Josefa, who had been standing there for ages, asked if she might go.

"No, you'll have to arrange everything, very discreetly, so that no one guesses. Get the boy to come here on Monday, around nine-thirty, when the master isn't here. Now listen carefully, Josefa, I don't want anyone to know a word of this."

"Don't worry, Madam. Almighty God and Our Lady are the only ones who've heard us."

Dona Laura's Lesson

THE YOUNG PEOPLE who were promoting the marriage never faltered in their propaganda and other preparations for the wedding, which they took very seriously. They went to see Dona Laura, to tell her that her godson's wedding day was not far off.

Dona Laura began to give Marajá some lessons in etiquette so that he would not let her down at the ceremony, and also to show the other white ladies that a black, given the proper education, could be a perfectly respectable person.

"Come on, Marajá, sit at the table, back straight now, don't slouch and elbows off the table. You pick up the soup spoon like this, and you drink from the sides of the spoon, not the front. Do you follow me?"

"Yes, I get it," Marajá laughed.

"You must not take too much alcohol and make a fool of yourself."

"You know I don't drink, Godmother."

"Yes, I know, but you'll have some champagne at the wedding reception. This is how you drink the toast... Come on, pick up your glass and clink it against mine: Chin-chin... very good, did you know how to do it already?"

"Of course I did, I've often helped out at the parties in the club, and served drinks in Sr Pinto's house."

"Fine, that brings me to my next point. Just now you mentioned Sr Pinto. From now on you're to call him father-in-law. You are his first son-in-law, you'll be making a rooster out of a chicken. Now, what else?... the napkin goes here, on your front or on your lap, here... When you wipe your lips, do so carefully, like me." Here she demonstrated. "Don't scrape your cutlery on the plate, eat slowly and quietly. Don't gulp your food down, don't put too much food in your mouth, and don't eat up everything, always leave a little on your plate. Never lick your plate, as you people do at home. Let me think... in church you have to do this, and when you sit at table, that." (All these instructions were accompanied by actions.) "The bride goes on this side." So she went on advising him on every minute detail, in twice-weekly sessions which made Sr Felix roar with laughter whenever he was present.

One afternoon, Dona Laura made her godson slip on a dinner-suit and white gloves borrowed from Sr Felix, to see how he would look on his wedding day. To increase the effect, she fetched Dona Sofia to stand in for the bride. The young man looked splendid, tall, strong and athletic. "Oh, he's impeccable, an absolutely first-class appearance! Stand back, boys and girls, and admire this young man in his dinner-suit, he looks like a Member of Parliament, or an Ambassador presenting his credentials in the highest diplomatic spheres!" The women were screaming with laughter, enjoying themselves. The lesser servants from the two households came into see the rehearsal—what a show! Dressing well is a gift, and Marajá looked superb. His godmother taught him to smile discreetly: "This is how you must appear before your bride and guests."

They put some records on the gramophone, a waltz and

a tango, but they need not have worried, Marajá was in his element. He glided forward, did turns, reverse turns and *chassés* in a way that left his godmother wide-eyed with admiration, so much so that she rewarded him with two big kisses! When it came to the tango, Dona Sofia had to give up before the end and confess she was profoundly moved, overwhelmed, even, because she had only ever known one man who could dance the tango so well, and that was her first suitor, and husband, who had died fifteen years previously in a car accident, on the very day of their wedding, when they were driving home after the ceremony. "This is the first time I've danced since then..."

Dona Laura went on with the lesson, showing Marajá how to invite a lady to dance, how to dance in a well-bred fashion, how to conduct a lady back to her seat. None of this was new to Marajá, for he had observed it all at the great banquets where he served the food and drinks.

"Marajá, I'm quite sure now you won't let me down, no matter how exalted the company, even with the wife of the Governor-General. Don't you agree, Dona Sofia?"

"Indeed I do, he even made me cry. But of course, blacks are born dancers, just look at the negroes in Brazil and Latin America."

Dona Laura's servants, who were present at the rehearsal, began to feel envious of Marajá. When they went back to their tasks, they were bored and disinclined to work. One of them spoke to the cook:

"I tell you this, José, I swear I'm not coming in on the day of the wedding, because I've no intention of putting up with a rabble. Have I to start serving Marajá, and him just a caretaker, because suddenly he's the boss's godson? Not me," said Lenga.

"I'm none too pleased myself, because if they hold the reception here in the house, the blacks from the shanty-towns will cause all sorts of trouble, as usual, once they get drunk. They'll start to fight, smash glasses and plates, and steal the cutlery and all the boss's liquor. I'm going to ask the mistress to see if it can't be held elsewhere."

"So what happens, José? Does this mean Marajá's going to be a big shot in the house? Is he going to be our boss? I remember we used to give him food here in the kitchen when he brought the boss's mail, and now he's going to order us around? No way."

"Forget it, he's going around saying he's going to marry a white man's daughter, but the whites will kill him. He'll be found one morning floating out there in the bay, you mark my words!..."

The servants were interrupted by the cries of the fish-wives walking through the street with their baskets on their heads, calling their wares:

"Fresh fish, fresh fish, who wants lovely fresh fish?" They wore clean cotton skirts and swung through the streets with their own peculiar sway of the hips, turning the streets into a theatre as their melodious cries rang through every district of the city.

"Come buy my fish, best-quality fresh fish!"

One woman who was a bit quicker than the others ran in front to capture the regular customers, or anyone who had not managed to get down to the market in Soki.

"Ladies, come see my ripe, juicy oranges... tangerines today, lovely and sweet," sang out a fruit-vendor on the other side of the street, a pretty woman with a basket on her head full of fruit from Loje. As she sold her fruit, she gave her customers a pleasant smile, showing off lovely white teeth, thanks to her efforts with a twig and the mixture of salt and soot that takes the place of Colgate.

"Oh, Cook and Lenga," Dona Laura called, "go and see what fish they're selling."

"Over, here, come and show us your fish and fruit,"

"Who, us?"

"Yes, you two."

"Oh, I hate going to that house," muttered the fish-wife to the fruit-vendor, "the woman always haggles about the price, she must think we just go down to the beach and find these beauties."

"Fish, lovely fresh fish, who'll buy?"

Visits

JOSEFA reminded her mistress that she had to go and see the witch doctor, as time was passing. Dona Amélia did not like the idea of going out amongst all those blacks. "I'll go instead," volunteered Josefa, though Joaquim doubted it would work. He thought it had to be the mistress herself. "I'll convince the witch doctor I'll do instead," Josefa promised. The best time to go would be the afternoon, then the cook could leave the dinner all prepared. The only problem was transport.

"Don't worry, the Bishop's chauffeur will be here soon and he's going to pick up some suckling pigs and ducks," said Dona Amélia.

"That's fine," Josefa agreed, "the witch doctor's place is near the farm, so he can give us a lift."

The chauffeur arrived, and with him Father José Maria, the Bishop's Secretary, in civilian dress, that is, shorts and a shirt, outrageous, but he argued that it was very hot. He often dressed like this when he was going for a ride, despite criticism from parishioners, colleagues and the Bishop himself. He had a poor reputation as a priest, being a bit of a Don Juan, but he was very good at looking after Church finances. He was going along with the chauffeur to choose a lamb as a present for the husband of one of his lady-friends.

Just as they were about to leave, a second luxurious car drew up, with the initials GG (Governor-General) on the door.

"I've been sent by Captain Melo, private secretary to the Governor, to see if you can fix him up with a baby goat and tell him how much it is, and...and... excuse me, Dona Amélia, but as I'm here could I ask you... I've been looking for ages for a suckling pig for my son's birthday party... would you mind?"

"Not at all, if you have the time, go along with the Father's car and you can take your pick."

"I certainly will, Dona Amélia, thank you very much," said the chauffeur, removing his cap and bowing.

"Could you possibly take my servants along? They have some business of their own to attend to in that area."

"Why, certainly, Dona Amélia, it will be a pleasure. Climb aboard."

"No, no," said Father José, "Josefa goes with me."

"Not another word, Father," said the Governor's driver, "I'll take the boy."

The two cars zoomed off past Bém-bém, heading for what is now the Golf Club, though at that time it was just bush and pasture. Old Joaquim kept looking out of the window, hoping to see someone who knew him so that he could wave to them from the Governor's car. No luck!

"Fancy me in the Governor's car, I've really come up in the world. This is the life, all right," he whispered to himself. He could not sit still, but hopped from one side of the seat to the other. The chauffeur had put him in the back in case the jolting of the car might bring his nice, white uniform with its gold buttons into contact with the cook's smelly clothes.

"Listen, why are you jumping from side to side like a

monkey in a cage?''

"I wasn't comfortable on that side."

"Honestly, you people, you're in the Governor's car and still you complain. Next thing you'll want out for a pee or to be sick?"

"No, sir, it's quite all right."

They were passing under cashew trees, and beneath the wheels they could feel the undulations of the sandy road out to Sr Pinto's pigsties and henruns.

In the Bishop's car, which had on the door the letters DCM (Director of Catholic Missions), the priest was trying to find out about the scandal. He was a friend of the family, in fact he aroused some suspicion, because he was never away from the house and was always to be seen in the company of Dona Amélia, or the eldest daughter, who had been packed off to Portugal. The housekeeper said nothing about the witch doctor. She was on her way to visit a sick uncle: there was no need for the Father to stop on his way back, they would catch a lift, there were always cars passing.

When they arrived at the turn-off, the witch doctor's hut could be clearly seen, about thirty metres from the main road. Beneath the cashew and mango trees stood cars and buses, four at the moment, whose occupants were consulting the master. When the two cars drew near, they attracted the attention of the people sitting in the shade of the cashews, who stood up to get a better view. Joaquim could not get the door open, so the chauffeur got out, removing his cap to cool his head a bit, and opened the door to let the cook out. Then the cars drove on. Imagine the comments:

"Good Lord, fancy the Governor-General's car coming here! And did you see that old black fellow in the back and how the white chauffeur held the door open for him, cap in hand? He must be a big shot, that old man, somebody really important…''

"Did you see the initials on the car?'' GG—Gangsters Galore.''

"Yes, all we need now is the Provincial Governor: PGL, Pack of Gangsters of Luanda.''

"But there was another car in front with DCM—that's the car from the Bishop's Palace. Don't tell me the Bishop wants the witch doctor to bless his statues. That would be a miracle!''

"You see, Domingos, you're always claiming the witch doctor's no good, yet even the whites from the government and the Church come to him. They send their servants by day, but by night they come themselves!''

It was Josefa and Joaquim's turn to go in. The old shaman was annoyed with the delegation from the Pinto household, because he needed the lady herself and had made that clear. Josefa tried to reason with him in Portuguese, which only made him all the more furious:

"Don't come speaking the white man's language. You're black and cannot stand in for a white person, it's no good. One of these days, you're going to have to stop fooling around. When I say I need the white lady, I mean the white lady. If you do this again, I'll put a nemorage (haemorrhage) on you from which you'll never get better. Don't say another word, off you go and tell your mistress to come here, that she won't be the first great lady I've seen.'' Turning to the cook, he added:

"You know me, you've been here often enough, I don't know how you could let this mistake happen. Go home, and don't come back without your mistress. Tell her I can do the business, but only if she comes herself.''

Josefa went outside, nervous and sweating with fear. A few seconds later, she felt herself wet down below.

''Oh, my God, it's my period and it's not even the right time! How did that happen?''

Terrified, she ran behind the witch doctor's pigsty to fix herself up. She was shaking, and did not go back to work that day. Next day, it was all over. ''Curse that old medicine man,'' she thought, crossing herself.

A week later, at nightfall, Dona Amélia went to the witch doctor. Josefa stayed in the car, Joaquim took his mistress inside and introduced her and then he, too, waited outside. Dona Amélia was unrecognisable, in African dress and with a kerchief on her head. The witch doctor made her remove the kerchief and one or two items of clothing, to make sure it was not sly-boots Josefa, as Dona Amélia's children called her. It all went very well, Dona Amélia reported happily when she came out.

A few days after these events, Marajá received a summons from Dona Amélia, through Josefa, who reassured him that it was just to ask him one or two little questions. Marajá was well acquainted with Josefa, for he had often delivered correspondence by hand for Sr Pinto to sign. So he knew the tricks Josefa got up to, stirring up trouble among the other servants to secure her own position as second-in-command of the household. Marajá did not like her, and besides, he knew it was she who had discovered Arlete's stained clothing and caused all the unpleasantness.

He agreed to go, nevertheless, and informed his godmother, who was delighted. She immediately called her neighbour to tell her the latest, that Marajá was to pay his first visit to the Pinto house as a future son-in-law.

"Good for my godson! This should take the Pintos down a peg or two! You go, my boy, and behave yourself, show you're a well-bred person, don't let me down. Oh, I'm so happy, Dona Sofia, it's full steam ahead now. Marajá, wear the suit the son of the manager of the insurance company gave you, you look nice in it."

At the appointed time, Marajá stood at the front gate and clapped his hands to be admitted to Arlete's parents' home.

"Oh, it's you, Marajá," said Josefa with a smile, "have you forgotten where the bell is?"

"Sometimes I don't like to ring, it can give people a scare. If the light's bad..."

"Very well, come in, come in. You look neat and smart and you've very polite all of a sudden. What's got into you?"

He was shown into a little study belonging to the lady of the house, where she sometimes wrote letters, but more often pondered all the business or other problems that might threaten the social position of the family. Following the witch doctor's instructions, Dona Amélia came in wreathed in smiles, though it cost her an effort. Marajá stood up, mindful of his godmother's lessons. You do not offer your hand to a superior or a married lady, you wait for them to do so, if they wish.

"Hello, Marajá, you're looking very grown-up and handsome, aren't you? I believe you're staying with Sr Felix, an excellent person. Such a pity I don't seem able to hit it off with his wife. You've filled out and you look very smart. How is the ping-pong and tennis coaching going?"

"I don't think I've put on any weight, Dona Amélia, I feel just the same. I've been practising out on the Island with some foreign gentlemen..."

Between them sat a small table with two glasses. One of them was intended for the visitor and held a potion from the witch doctor to change the audacious fellow's mind.

"I asked you here in order to find out if the rumours I have heard are true, that you're still seeing Miss Arlete?... Oh, do have some fruit-juice," said Dona Amélia, offering the visitor his glass.

"I must confess, Dona Amélia, that I haven't seen Arlete again and I don't know if..."

At this point, in came Sr Pinto, who had come back because he had forgotten the key to his desk. Josefa had no chance to warn them, she just collapsed against the wall with her hands over her ears, waiting for the explosion. He strode into the room: Boooom!

"What the devil is going on, Amélia?" he bellowed at the top of his voice. "This is outrageous, I'm doing my best to arrange everything, and my own wife is sitting at home entertaining this nuisance, this animal. I'll kill him, I swear!"

"Oh, Pinto, don't do anything foolish. Help, Josefa, quick!"

While Pinto was running to the bedroom to get his pistol, Marajá took advantage of the opportunity to sneak into the yard (he knew every nook and cranny of the house) and run off. He came across Joaquim emptying a drum of bleach near the yard wall, which was high and had no steps, so he put his hands on the old man's shoulders (Joaquim barely realised what was going on), leap-frogged over the wall and came flying down on the other side, vrooom, his jacket billowing out like a parachute, an Olympic-style high-jump, never before seen off the sports field...

"Stop, thief!" Old Joaquim was not too frightened to call for help, his cries of alarm blending with the din from the

Pintos' bedroom. Josefa was grappling with Sr Pinto, trying to grab the pistol and Dona Amélia was weeping and begging Pinto to listen to her explanation. Everything was turned upside down. What a shambles! Glasses, candlesticks, cups and saucers, everything that had been set out on the centre table or on little side tables lay smashed in pieces on the waxed floor, like confetti and rice after a wedding.

Marajá was not sure whether Josefa and Dona Amélia had drawn him into a trap with the intention of killing him. He ran home in great fright and confusion, his clothes dishevelled. On arrival at his godmother's house, he told her the whole story to Dona Laura's astonishment and indignation. She roundly cursed Dona Amélia, despite Marajá's insistence that Arlete's mother had to some extent received him kindly.

When his fury had died down, Sr Pinto was sorry that his wife had not kept him abreast of her plans, for he could have helped her to persuade the boy to change his mind and leave Angola.

A Play of Marriage

THE PROMOTERS of the marriage gradually began to tire, but then, as it was Carnival time, they had another idea: to produce a play in which Marajá and Arlete would be the main characters. This was the plan: one Saturday afternoon, they would hire taxis and form a cortège at the same time as some wedding in the Cathedral. This they would attend as though they were guests or onlookers. Then a reception would be held at Sr Felix and Dona Laura's house, and they would play the part of the groom's godparents. The students would pay to have all the church-bells rung, especially by the acrobat who was in charge of the bells at the Carmo Church. There would be a ball with ladies and gentlemen dressed in appropriate costume. All the important people from the government and business milieux would be invited and it would be they who met the expenses. Everything was got ready, the script was written and it was all organised so that everyone knew his part, except for one or two details which were to be kept secret and surprise everyone on the actual day. The date was fixed.

Dona Laura refused to have the reception in her garden; apart from the inconvenience, she did not want to get on the wrong side of Dona Amélia. She advised them to hold the performance in some club frequented by their parents, or somewhere else indoors. This was agreed, and they booked the Guild, though some were not keen on this venue, thinking it was too public. (The Guild stood where the Kuale Restaurant is today, facing the Largo do Alfândega, now the Land Survey Offices.)

It was Saturday afternoon, the day before the start of Carnival, and Luanda was in a whirl, full of people and cars, the noise of whistles, streamers, and a general festive atmosphere. It was a pleasant afternoon, not too hot, despite the time of year. It had rained a little early in the morning, as is traditional at Carnival time. Everything was ready. A group of students had checked that nothing had been forgotten. Enquiries had been made at all the churches and sacristans bribed with money, clothes, and sweets to ensure that all the bells rang out at exactly five p.m. for ten minutes. There was a double bribe for the fellow at the Carmo Church, for he had a larger part, he had to ring the bells for fifteen minutes. If any sacristans or bell-ringers made difficulties, they were shown an authorisation on headed notepaper from the Archbishop's Palace, duly stamped and with scribbled signature. Any further doubts were removed by one of the group dressed as a priest.

The pretty girls who had been chosen as maids of honour looked bewitching and they had happily rehearsed their roles in Gioconda's house. Arlete was got ready at the home of Manuela, a friend from school who had come to an arrangement with the housekeeper while her parents were on holiday in Portugal. The housekeeper had ample experience of weddings, for it was she who dressed the brides in big society weddings. They told her not to worry, it was just for Carnival, she would not get into trouble.

Taxis had been hired from the ranks, and the students were

also using their parents' cars. No expense was spared, this was to be a wedding to remember. They had found out there were two marriages being celebrated in the Carmo Church, two in the Cathedral, one in the Immaculate Conception and two in St Paul's, as well as a christening in the church of Nazareth. A large number of people were sent invitations to the play, at six o'clock, in the place indicated, to be followed by a dance. Black ties for the gentlemen, long dresses for the ladies, entrance by invitation only. Father Angelo, chaplain to the armed forces, an open-minded and jolly young man, offered to help with the festivities.

The cars were lined up and set off, with streamers flying from the windows and children running alongside, for the Cathedral, where a large crowd of students was waiting, on the alert for possible trouble with the police.

There were loud hurrahs for the bride and the maids of honour as they stepped out of the cars. A policeman came over and asked the students to make less noise, as the Cathedral was not the place for Carnival pranks. They swallowed that in silence. Some more people came running up, for it was unusual to hear such loud hurrahs. The young people cleared a space in front of the steps leading up to the main entrance to the Cathedral. The maids of honour were like splendid doves in their silk and tafetta dresses, flowers and veils. Arlete was like an angel, far surpassing the painting of the Saint opposite the altar. The guests for the next wedding, who were already inside the church, stood up to take a look, and those from the previous ceremony, who had finished and were now on their way out, also stopped, in fact the groom was so busy staring at Arlete on the best man's arm that he quite forgot about his own new bride.

Actually, the groom who was seated should have been

married first, but his bride had still not appeared, so there he waited, with his relatives and guests around him. When they saw the crowd arriving with Arlete, they assumed it must be his bride. Arlete sat down with her train of followers on the first row of seats inside the door, and the priest announced:

"Well, now the bride has arrived, let us begin the ceremony, with apologies for the late start, but it was not our fault." He beckoned for Arlete and her friends to approach the altar, but the groom looked up and shook his head as if to say, "No, no, it's not the right one." The godparents and relatives of the absent bride went up to the priest and whispered in his ear. A few ladies murmured that the groom should take what he was being offered... what a lovely girl!... anyone would envy her beauty... a real treasure.

The priest consulted his sacristan and confirmed that only two weddings were booked for that day. Fonseca, the producer of the play, lied convincingly that there had been some mistake, they were sure the marriage of Arlete and Marajá Miguel was due to take place there.

"No, no, I've only got two weddings: one I've just done, and the other is still waiting for the bride."

"Excuse us, Father, it must be in the Carmo Church."

"You mentioned the name Marajá Miguel? Is he Indian, Chinese, Arab or what?"

"He's black, Father, and Angolan."

"A black with a name like Marajá, which is not even Christian, and he's marrying that white girl? She is white, isn't she?"

"Yes, Father, she is. Excuse me, and sorry for the mix-up."

Fonseca signalled to his people to stand up, and announced in a loud voice that there had been a mistake, and it was in the Carmo Church. When they came out, the boys and girls threw flowers and rice at Arlete, who was on Fonseca's arm and the great bell began to vibrate and ring out its different peals. Off they went to the Carmo Church, just for a moment. All the bells of the city were ringing, each with its characteristic chime. The bell-ringer of the Carmo Church joined in: ding, ding, ding, Dongg...Donggg... The priest who was celebrating a wedding looked puzzled, and sent the sacristan to tell him to stop, it wasn't time. But what happened? The sacristan climbed up the ladder and grabbed the bell-ringer's leg, but he jerked away and landed the sacristan a terrible kick, and the bells rang even louder. Back went the sacristan and told the priest the bell-ringer had been possessed by the devil.

No-one ever rang a bell so rhythmically and so melodiously as this renowned bell-ringer of the Carmo Church. Young people in the streets, and the children in the mission, would dance to his *conga*, for he could ring to the rhythm of an African dance. He had special peals for weddings, funerals or baptisms. There was no one to touch him.

The procession wound its way through the streets to cries of "It's a wedding." Meanwhile, some friends of Arlete's parents thought they recognised her, and ran off to tell them for they could not believe that Pinto would marry his daughter with never a word to old friends, and as they had not seen him at the ceremony, they thought she must be getting married without his consent.

"Where did you see her?" asked Pinto in alarm.

"At the Cathedral, but I'm not sure it was her, it looked like her, dressed as a bride and with the priest just about to begin the ceremony."

Our friend Pinto lost no time in speeding to the Cathedral,

but of course the couple had already left. He spoke to the priest and the sacristan who assured him there was no such name in the register, but they did remember a bride who had made a mistake and gone from there to the Carmo Church. Despite the late hour, Pinto roused the priests there in order to find out the truth. Again he was assured that the wedding had not taken place there. His younger daughter suggested that Arlete had gone to the High School play, since that was what she had implied to her mother when she went out, adding she'd be home late.

When they decided to forget about a real wedding, the young people resolved that Marajá should go to the theatre, all dressed up to play the part of the groom, but that he should not go to the church, to avoid complications. Sr Pinto, who was already half-mad, might turn up and bash his brains out.

It was not easy to convince Marajá, either about the real wedding or, later, that he should take part in the play. "I refuse, I want nothing more to do with her, I've suffered enough already." However, they pressed him so much, especially his pupils from the tennis club, that he had to give in and agree to appear at the theatre, but only so as not to spoil the festivities and seem ungrateful for all the help and consideration he had been shown, and the solidarity offered by the students, who had stood by him when he needed it.

The marriage procession arrived at the Island and made its way to the reception room, which was decorated and ready. When all the other cars had gone in, the one in which the bride was riding stopped a hundred metres from the entrance. Out got Fonseca and in went Marajá, who had been waiting under a fig tree for the last two hours. The bridal car then drew up, amid honking horns, whistles, fireworks and enthusiastic cat-calls from the students:

Marajá, Marajá, ra, ra, ra,
She's great, you bet: Arlete, Arlete, Arlete.

When they went in, there was a huge display of fireworks. The ordinary inhabitants of the Island were astonished to see such celebration at a wedding, even in Carnival-time. The white man who lived next door could not believe his eyes when he saw the white girl arm-in-arm with the black man. People came from the shanty-town to see, and on the way back the children improvised a *samba*:

Mara, Mara, já, já, Mara, Mara, já, já,
Arlete, ete, ete, Arlete, ete, ete.

On this same day, the eve of Carnival, Josefa worked almost till nightfall, then said goodbye to Dona Amélia. She was not going home to the working-class area where she lived, but to the Island to pay a visit to an aunt and perhaps stay the night.

Josefa was good-looking, a haughty woman with a stand-offish air. She was always dressed in the latest style, for the ladies in the great houses where she had worked, and now Dona Amélia, gave her cast-offs. She was tall and still slim and as she walked through the cobbled street she filled them with the tap, tap, tapping of her high-heeled, pointed-toe shoes. She swung her hips as though she had been born and reared in one of the fashion centres of Europe. Recently she had taken to imitating the walk of Dona Celia, the pretty young wife, newly arrived from Portugal, of Lieutenant Fonseca, an officer attached to the Governor's Residence.

As she walked along, a loud procession of cars passed her—it was probably a wedding. They gave noisy hoots on their horns, apparently aimed at her, but she paid no attention,

143

keeping her eyes on the ground. Today she was wearing a close-fitting skirt and jacket in grey linen, with earrings and round her neck a gold chain with a charm in the shape of a heart. She wore two rings on her left hand, a fine silk shawl hung down her back, and she carried a black handbag under her arm. As she advanced she left in the air a strong perfume, which drove away the flies.

At nightfall, adults and children who had seen the cars arriving passed near Josefa's aunt's yard, commenting on their surprise and pleasure at the wedding of the black man and the pretty white girl. "She's like the angel in the church of Our Lady of the Cape, isn't she, Mingota?" The children were imitating the students' calls:

Marajá, Marajá, ra, ra, ra,.
She's great, you bet: Arlete, Arlete, Arlete.

The housekeeper was astonished at what she heard. Apprehensively, she asked a few questions, then a few more, seeking minute details that the girls could hardly supply. "Yes, he was black, all right, tall, handsome and dressed like a white man," they told her. "We couldn't really see the girl's face, she was wearing a veil and there were lots of other white girls around her. Santa was a bit nearer, she noticed she was very pretty. She was about the same size as Zinha, here, and with a figure like my aunt Violante. Isn't that so, Nina?"

"Yes, that's right."

There could be no doubt, Arlete had got married in secret, without even telling her parents. Oh, what a terrible shock for the family. She had seen Sr Pinto go out this afternoon in a great hurry, with another man, and heard them mention Arlete's name, but he was not away for long, and when he came back he looked normal, not angry at all, and he ate a hearty tea... What could it mean?

"Aunty, I'm just popping out for a minute. Children, come and show me the place."

A pretend wedding ceremony had taken place at the Guild, very well presented, with all the usual ritual of a church wedding. Unfortunately, this later brought down criticism, and even punishment, on the students who had taken part. Some were suspended from the school for a time, for offending against public morality and the dignity of the Church. Father Angelo, who had supervised the ceremony from a distance, was suddenly transferred to Portugal, with no right of appeal.

Josefa arrived just as the couple were entering the ball room. She was not allowed in, as she had no invitation. Anxious to make sure it really was Arlete and Marajá, she went sniffing around the yard looking for a way in, but with no luck, so she asked a neighbour whose yard overlooked the ballroom to let her take a look from his verandah. And there she spied Arlete in Marajá's arms, preparing to dance.

They led off with a tempestuous tango, which they had been rehearsing in a friend's house, and which left the spectators open-mouthed in admiration. There were calls for an encore, and the couple obliged. Never, not even in Argentina, birthplace of the tango, as they say, was it danced with such rhythm and such studied and calculated movements as Marajá and Arlete displayed on this occasion with the well-know airs, *Adiós, pampa mía* and *La cumparsita*.

Arlete, who a month before had not even known how to dance, whirled round the floor, her beauty set off to perfection by the long bridal-gown and the ornaments and jewels arranged by the clever hand of Manuela's housekeeper, Dona Susana, who was an expert at dressing brides, whether virgins or hags, in such a way that priests and ministers could barely keep their mind on their task as they officiated at the altar.

It is not done to ask the happy couple to repeat the first dance, but on this occasion the convention was ignored, so once again they glided over the wide cement floor, Arlete whirling round or bending over backwards, supported by Marajá's arm. Her dress ballooned out as she spun round, draping itself around Marajá in his impeccable navy suit and shoes which gleamed like fireflies. Arlete's jewels sparkled. A falling star from the direction of St Michael's Fort flew over the yard and fell into the murmuring sea. It was a lovely sight, homage to the young couple. The bride began to cry. "Hurrah for the bride and groom," some guests called.

The maids of honour came to console their emotional friend. Some caught the mood and began to cry themselves, while Marajá was greatly moved by the hugs and kisses he received from all the tennis-players. However, he made a great effort to smile happily and wave to his guests who kept up a ceaseless chant: "Hurrah for the bride and groom." Who would have thought it was just a scene from a play? It was a magnificent wedding, with all the little details and touches of a proper ceremony, and the guests ate, drank and danced till Sunday morning. Many people on their way back from other weddings that had taken place that day stopped by the Island, drawn by Gold-Tooth's discotheque and by the firework display laid on by the students. Everyone present took as many photographs as they wished of the different stages of the ceremony: exchanging the rings, signing the register and cutting the cake, Arlete with the organisers and with friends from school and the tennis club. Someone had the bright idea later of sending a complete set to Dona Laura, and another to Dona Amélia—surely the sight of Marajá embracing her daughter in a marriage ceremony would be enough to drive her aboard the *Mouzinho*.

Meanwhile the neighbours on the verandah next door were applauding in appreciation of the couple's prowess at the tango, when suddenly Josefa uttered the one word "Married!" and fell unconscious to the ground. Her eyes were open, she was foaming at the mouth and had wet herself. So much for her perfume!

"Help, help, get the driver of one of the wedding cars to take this woman to the hospital. What a dreadful thing to happen! I let her come on to my verandah, and here she is now, half-dead. What am I going to tell the police? What rotten luck, you never get a moment's peace in this miserable life," wailed the wife of the owner of the house, carrying the body to a car to be taken to the hospital. Few people at the dance realised what had happened, only one or two heard that the maid next door had fainted.

It was at this moment Tamoda arrived. He was exhausted from searching for Bangu and the place where the wedding was being held. He had gone from the native quarter to the club, and from there to Dona Laura's, with no luck. Bangu, for his part, had been trying without success since Friday to find his friend and tell him that the wedding was off. There was a student at the door as porter and from inside could be heard prolonged applause, cries of "Encore" and "Viva" and the noise of fireworks.

"Kindly allow me to enter."

"Have you an invitation?"

"No, but I'm to deliver the principal peroration at the nuptials."

"Why, who are you?"

"I must insist on being treated with reciprocal courtesy, not in this contumelious fashion."

"Good Lord, I don't understand a word you say. Is this a joke, or are you off your rocker? You've no invitation and you're causing a nuisance, do I make myself clear?"

"Allow me to repeat affirmatively that I am to be the principal speech-maker, at the explicit invitation of my friend, Bangu." Tamoda began to unroll the speech he had brought.

"Wait here."

The elegantly-dressed young man went off to make enquiries:

"Hey, Bangu, there's a black outside, a common fellow like yourself. Yet I can't understand a word he says. Come and see whether you know him."

"Why, Tamoda, here you are at last. I've been looking everywhere for you. I went to your cousin's house, but I couldn't find you..." Bangu turned to the porter:

"Let him in, José Maria, he's a friend of mine who was invited to say a few words if the wedding came off."

As they were crossing the threshold, Tamoda stared at José Maria and complained:

"I was declassified, reviled and intermittently insulted by this man, in a fashion hard to tolerate, even for a polymath like myself."

"Yes, I'm sorry about that. Let's go in. I'm afraid the wedding was called off, so we did a play instead, seeing it was Carnival. The boys organised everything..." said Bangu.

"But what about my speech?"

"You can't give it now, how can you if there's been no wedding?"

"That's neither here nor there, Bangu, I insist on my right to perform a speech, in view of the offensiveness penetrated against my honour by this white porter-fellow. I want to show him I can carry out a speech, and I cannot accept..."

"Tamoda, I'm going to get angry with you if you cause any trouble. All the boys here are students, educated people who won't stand for nonsense. Don't spoil the party. I feel it's all my fault. Wait here and I'll see what I can do."

Bangu went over to Fonseca and tapped him on the shoulder.

"I'm glad I've found you. I've got a bit of a problem with a friend who was invited to give a speech and has just turned up. Couldn't we find a space somewhere in the rest of the play for him to speak? He's come all the way from his village in my part of the country, and it'll look bad for me if..."

"I've no objection, but what will he say? You say he's come from a village, will he talk rubbish? You know there are a lot of important people here. Marajá wants to go, his part's finished and he's very worried in case Pinto turns up. Arlete wants to go as well, so if your friend is going to speak, it has to be now, and we'll ask them to wait for a minute. Let's have a look at the text."

The written speech was perfectly all right, so it was all arranged. Fonseca stopped the music and said they would now hear a few words on the subject of marriage, which as the ladies and gentlemen knew, was traditional at wedding receptions. Some of the organisers objected to an unknown black stepping in at the last moment and altering the programme by making a speech. "It doesn't matter." "Yes, it does." "Oh, let him do it." "No, I won't." However, finally a consensus was reached, thanks to a Major who was also a teacher in the school, an elderly man, but a great friend of the youngsters. Also, some of the ladies present were curious to hear the unknown black speak. And it was quite true, some guests added, that a speech was needed to complete the proceedings.

Tamoda was led to the spot and introduced as a friend of Bangu and Marajá. He was wearing a nice suit, with a stiff collar and tie and he had brylcreemed his hair. He ran his finger round the edge of his collar, Once, twice, then he began:

Cherished and illustrious bride and groom,

It is with deep and sincere emotion that I address you on the threshold of your journey together as Christian man and wife. Allow me, as an elder brother, to remind you of certain truths which will be like lamps illuminating your lives together. Marriage is a natural institution, pleasing to God, who at the dawn of creation formed Man in His Own image, and so that he would not be lonely, He gave him a companion like unto himself, as we read in the Book of Genesis. Marriage was elevated to the sacrament of Holy Matrimony by Jesus Christ, Our Lord...

"Exactly. Very well put," could be heard from the mouths of several guests. There was a long round of applause. One old lady made the sign of the cross, and the old Major walked right up to Tamoda, took off his spectacles and stared hard at the orator's face, then shook his head and murmured:

"Wonderful speech, that's a very intelligent black."

Tamoda continued in measured tones, his voice ringing with emotion:

This sacred union, which makes of man and woman one flesh, is indissoluble, and consent, once given, can not be withdrawn: 'What God has brought together let no man put asunder' as the gospel tells us...

"Well spoken, very well spoken. Pity it's only a speech in a play. If only it could be heard by all young people, and by those wicked husbands who neglect their wives or give them a hard life," said several guests.

"That black has a good head on his shoulders," approved another.

"He's probably an ex-seminarist," pronounced some ladies with satisfaction.

Tamoda cleared his throat, to indicate that he was about to begin again:

> The union of man and wife is indissoluble, because it is a symbol of the divine union between God and Man, and between Jesus Christ and His Church, which the Apostle tells us is one of the great mysteries...

Tumultuous applause. One old woman requested that when the man finished speaking, he should be brought to her for a kiss, "even if he is black, it doesn't matter."

"From the way he speaks, he must have been training for the priesthood, he knows the Holy Scriptures inside out," the other ladies insisted.

Now, Tamoda was not one for reading his speeches to an audience, especially if he had not written them himself. He preferred to use his own words, so with two pages still to go, he gathered up those he had read, folded them and put them to one side, while he waited for the approbation and applause his speech had aroused to die down. He nodded his head, smiling at the audience, and when he began again he was improvising:

> My dear Bride and Bridegroom,
> Honoured Guests,
> Ladies and Gentlemen gathered here together at this most sumptuary of matrimonial proceedings: I am certain that the two young people now joined as one

151

are not examples of such debauchery or licentiousness as to disauthorize the arguments already brought forth with appropriate erudition. Man and wife, whatever they may discover about each other, must love, honour and obey in accordance with the hypotenuse of this happy day. Even if the one should turn out to have no hair down below, or the other notices his horns beginning to grow, there should be no complaint. Even if the bridegroom spots the absence of the precious flower of vir...

Just as he was about to complete the word "virginity", all the lights went out.

"What on earth happened to the man? He started off so well, now he's talking utter nonsense! Dona Zulmira, have you any idea what's going on?"

"None at all, I'm baffled."

Similar whispered comments could be heard from all sections of the disillusioned audience.

"Just keep the lights off, to shut him up, and we can all go home," someone suggested to the organisers.

However, there were two distinct groups in the hall. One, the guests of honour, consisted of outstanding figures in the social and political life of the colony, and they occupied the main tables. The other consisted of chauffeurs, shop-assistants, cooks, servants, waiters, a few curious spectators who had been allowed in, and the workman who had built and painted the installations. This second group had no tables, but ate and drank standing up or sitting on the sandy ground in the yard. They applauded everything with great liveliness and enthusiasm, clapping more and more loudly as the night advanced and the pile of empty wine and beer bottles grew higher in a corner of the yard.

From time to time, there would be cries and applause from this part of the crowd that had nothing to do with the ceremony. Sometimes one of the organisers would go over and ask them to keep the noise down, "Otherwise you're out!" While Tamoda was reading the first part of his speech, there was no response from them, but they brightened up at the improvisation, which to their mind was the best part— "very meaty!"

Despite the efforts made by some guests to have Tamoda stopped, he was able to continue with his speech:

Dear Bride and Groom,
Honoured Ladies,
Revered Gentlemen:

This nuptial union is born of the voluptuous desire of the bride and groom, who met, liked each other and eventually fell in love. Therefore we as honoured guests are gathered here to celebrate this happy couplement. All those who enter into the state of matrimony must respect their partner's defectuosities. Even if the expected pearl of virginity is missing, even if there is hairlessness in an awkward place, they should be understanding and comprehensive, because...

Here he was interrupted:

"Throw that man out, he's talking rubbish and besides, it's an insult, insinuating things like that about the bride. This black is taking advantage of a bit of carnival play-acting to offend distinguished people, founders of this colony and representatives of Portugal. This is the limit!"

"Throw out the drunk instead, he's the one talking rubbish. Carry on, Sr Tamoda, you're doing okay." This was accompanied by applause and cries of "Hear, hear," from the humbler members of the audience. Tamoda, who until now had stayed mute, grew bolder. He looked at the audience and the happy couple and continued:

Noble Lords and Ladies,
Honoured Guests:
I am dumbfounded by the innuendoings of that jackanapes.

"Never mind him, he was drunk, he's gone now, carry on..."

Tamoda straightened his tie, stretched his neck, and again began to speak in his own inimitable way:

"Never have I been an ocular witness to more joyful or more pleasurable matrimonials, for normally white marries white, here we have the unusual sight of white bride and black groom..."

"Here, here, very good, long live Marajá and his bride!"

"Hip, hip, hurrah!"

"To the newly-weds!"

"Carry on, black brother, make us proud!" shouted one the servants who was drunk.

"I shall end," said Tamoda, "by wishing them a libidinous wedding-night and in the near future many offsprings. I beg pardon if I have been over-locquacious."

There was prolonged applause, loud cheers, cries of "Chin-chin" and clinking of glasses. Amid this din, some people were killing themselves laughing:

"What a marvellous show, really colourful and original! That was a superb orator the students found!"

"Ho, ho, ho," cried one man, slapping his thighs, "I never laughed so much in all my life."

"Jorge, what does 'libidinous' mean?"

"I'm not sure, but since he mentioned offspring I think

it means lots of kissing and cuddling."

"Ho, ho, ho, I've got a stitch from laughing", a man said, holding his sides. "Where on earth did they dig up that amazing black fellow? You only see things like that on the stage. What an astonishing chap, I'm sore all over."

"He's not from around here, they brought him in from his village, he's a friend of Bangu and Marajá."

"He's certainly got a way with him, he's quite a character, I nearly died laughing."

Another guest began to imitate Tamoda:

"Ladies and gentleforks..."

A burst of laughter was heard from a group of men in a corner with glasses in their hands, who had thoroughly enjoyed the main speaker and were now imitating his manner. Some could not remain upright any longer, and sprawled instead on the white sand, which does not stain your clothing. Others still were mocking the matron of honour, a black woman with very poor manners, who was as drunk as a lord, and belched every few seconds.

What happened was that Bangu originally persuaded a pretty black girl, Zina, to take on this role. It was all arranged, but when they went to collect her they found she had been taken to hospital the night before. There was no time to find another girl, but as Bangu was on his way home through the working-class district he bumped into a good-time girl he used to know, an ugly woman, very fond of a drink.

"Come on Rosa, I've got a little job for you out on the Island."

"What sort of job, Bangu? Is it a bunch of sailors?"

"Nothing like that. Off you go home and put on a nice dress and a pair of shoes. I'll take you to a wedding, but make it snappy. You're the matron of honour."

"Slow down, you know what they say, the more hurry, the less speed. For a start, I've no papers, how can I go to the church?"

"Don't worry about that, just come along. There are no papers at this wedding."

"No papers? How come? Is this a proper wedding, or some kind of joke, Bangu?"

As they walked along, he explained what was happening, how she was to play her part, the sort of people who would be there, and what she must and must not do. Alas, she did not behave herself, despite Bangu's advice and her own vast experience as matron of honour at her god-daughters' weddings. Seated at the main table, she never let her glass remain empty, for she would always beckon a waiter, "Fill'er up!" She talked nineteen to the dozen and emitted frequent loud belches like a constipated foghorn. Several times, she interrupted Tamoda's speech with an ill-timed "Hear, hear." Some matron of honour! Bangu was bitterly ashamed, and could not wait to bundle her off in the early hours of the morning.

"I asked Bangu to get us a nice, pretty black girl for the matron of honour, one of the students would have done, it was just to plug a gap. Where on earth did he dig up that ugly brute. Ugh!" complained one of the organisers.

"You must admit it did not put Tamoda off his stride, he just said: 'The person who is emitting belchings should be expulsed.' "

"No, he said something like: 'I demand that the person who is emitting loud belchings should be expulsed by Bangu, immediately, if not sooner.' "

"I'll tell you one thing, it was the black fellow that really made the play a success."

"I quite agree. I loved the bit where he had the nerve to talk about the bride being pregnant."

A newcomer came over to join the wagging tongues. He had been sitting at the bridal table with all the big-wigs.

"Heard the latest? It turns out Mestre Tamoda didn't know the whole thing was just a play, he thought it was the real thing."

"You don't say! I bet he was wild when he found out, and wished he hadn't done it. That was a rotten trick to play on the poor devil."

"Why? It turned out to be a first-class spectacle."

"True, and a big joke on Arlete's parents."

"Let it be a lesson to them. Their daughter got her own back, it's just a pity they weren't at the show. In fact, it should be a lesson to everyone who was there, all the high and mighty, the snobs..."

Some of the guests of honour had begun to leave when Tamoda began his improvised speech. Marajá and Arlete left a little later, so they missed the fun when the party was invaded in the early hours of the morning by gatecrashers who joyfully carried on the Carnival dance.

ABOUT THE TRANSLATOR. Annella McDermott comes from Glasgow and studied modern languages at the University of Glasgow, 1962-67. Since 1969 she has been a lecturer in the Department of Hispanic, Latin American and Portuguese Studies at the University of Bristol. She has a special interest in Latin American literature and has also translated a biography of Simón Bolívar.